THE INSISTENT

The

INSISTENT
CALL

Rhetorical Moments
in Black Anticolonialism,

1929–1937

ARIC PUTNAM

University of Massachusetts Press
Amherst and Boston

LC 2012026784

ISBN 978-1-55849-978-2 (paper); 977-5 (hardcover)

Designed by Steve Dyer
Set in Garamond Premier Pro
Printed and bound by Thomson-Shore, Inc.

LIBRARY OF CONGRESS CATALOGING-IN-PUBLICATION DATA

Putnam, Aric, 1972–

The insistent call : rhetorical moments in black anticolonialism, 1929–1937 /
Aric Putnam.

p. cm.

Includes bibliographical references and index.

ISBN 978-1-55849-978-2 (pbk. : alk. paper) —
ISBN 978-1-55849-977-5 (library cloth : alk. paper)

1. African Americans—Race identity—History—20th century.
2. African Americans—Attitudes—History—20th century.   3. African diaspora.
4. Anti-imperialist movements—United States—History—20th century.
5. Rhetoric—Political aspects—United States.
6. American prose literature—African American authors—History and criticism.
7. Haiti—History—American occupation, 1915–1934—Social aspects.
8. Labor movement—Liberia—History—20th century.
9. Italo-Ethiopian War, 1935–1936—Social aspects.   I. Title.

E185.625 .P
305.896'0730904—dc23
2012026784

British Library Cataloguing in Publication data are available.

FOR

Robert H. Putnam

(1944–2008)

CONTENTS

ACKNOWLEDGMENTS

WHEN I THINK of these words appearing in print I am inclined to pinch myself, not only because clearly I need waking up, but also because a good pinch would remind me how it feels to write a book.

All scholarly labor is collective and so was this project. My collective begins with Kirt Wilson, who has been a great adviser and an even better friend. The book also benefited from the advice and insight of my graduate school teachers, especially Karlyn Kohrs Campbell, Ed Schiappa, Nate Stormer, and John S. Wright. This project is also indebted to my good friends and colleagues who have read bits of this work and provided feedback and support—namely, Terry Check, Jeremy Engels, Eric Fuchs, Joshua Gunn, Martin Lang, Shane Miller, Christopher Swift, and Steve Thomas.

I thank Brian Halley for soliciting the project and gracefully guiding it to completion, and Barbara Folsom and the fine folks at University of Massachusetts Press for improving it along the way.

Last, Laurie, Eliza, and Phineas (but especially Laurie), this is your fault. You are the reason I started this and, more important, the reason I finished it. Thank you.

Parts of chapters 4 and 5 were previously published in *Rhetoric and Public Affairs* (Michigan State Press) and are used here with their kind permission:

Aric Putnam, "Ethiopia Is Now: J. A. Rogers and the Rhetoric of Black Anti-colonialism during the Great Depression," *Rhetoric and Public Affairs* 10.3 (2007): 421–46; and "'Modern Slaves': The Liberian Labor Crisis and the Politics of Race and Class." *Rhetoric and Public Affairs* 9.2 (2006): 235–56.

THE INSISTENT CALL

Rhetoric and Diaspora

I N 1924, AT A C I V I C C L U B gathering to celebrate Jessie Fauset's book *There Is Confusion,* Alain Locke was asked to edit a special issue of *Survey Graphic* magazine. Locke's objective was to shed light on African America's Harlem and to document the sociological and artistic developments that were creating a "black mecca" in a New York neighborhood.[1] The result of his labors, eventually published as *The New Negro: An Interpretation,* has been considered the "first national book" of black America and the "Bible" of the New Negro Movement, the loose collective of social and cultural elites who debated black identity in the 1920s.[2]

Countee Cullen's poem "Heritage" was situated in the center of Locke's anthology, in the middle of the section titled "The Negro Digs up His Past," between the folktale "B'rer Rabbit Fools Buzzard" and Locke's own paean to African aesthetics, "Legacy of the Ancestral Arts."[3] The poem, like much black cultural and political discourse during this period, was both intensely personal and public, critical of yet deeply invested in history, modern and traditional at the same time. In "Heritage" a young artist struggles to reconcile what his past suggests he is with what he feels he should become.

The poem begins by questioning the nature and value of the poet's "African" heritage. The poet asks "What is Africa to me?" and then rephrases the question and hazards an answer: "Copper sun, a scarlet sea / Jungle star and jungle track / Strong bronzed men and regal black / Women from whose loins I sprang / When the birds of Eden sang?" Rephrasing the opening question a third time, the stanza continues, expressing a resigned, indifferent attitude toward Africa: "One three centuries removed / From the scenes his fathers loved / Spicy grove and banyan tree / What is Africa to me?" The repetition and casual framing of the question suggests fatigue, as if the question were too often asked or the poem's narrator feels no imperative to find the right answer. Regardless, the poet is clearly ambivalent about more than Africa; he is indifferent to his past—his genetic, familial, cultural foundation. The second stanza of the poem states this ambivalence unambiguously: "Africa? A book one thumbs / Listlessly until slumber comes."[4]

Still, even though the poet characterizes Africa as "unremembered," he concedes that it shapes his behavior; the poem describes it as a natural space where desire survives in a purer state than in the modern condition. In Africa, young "forest lovers lie / Plighting troth beneath the sky." Africa is primitive, preconscious, prelapsarian. As such, it is also irrepressible, as the poet reports: "So I lie, who always hear / Though I cram against my ear / Both my thumbs, and keep them there, / Great drums beating through the air." Despite his ambivalence and his other priorities, Africa persists in the poet's identity, resurfacing as a metaphor for fundamental desires and a mythic respite from alienation.

The final section of the poem laments the irreconcilability of ideals and reality, African heritage and "American" actuality. The poem argues, "Heathen gods are naught to me— / Quaint, outlandish heathen gods / Black men fashion out of rods, / Clay and brittle bits of stone, / In a likeness of their own." These lines suggest the poet's alienation from Africa, as the "likeness" of these "heathen" gods is obviously foreign to the poet's image of himself; however, within the context of the poem, this passage also implies envy. Africans gods grow from and reflect the experiences of African people. The Christian god, in contrast, is ignorant of the authentic alienation that black Christians have known: "Must my heart grow sick and falter / Wishing He I served were black / Thinking then it would not lack / Precedent of pain to guide it." The poet suggests that African religion may be "heathen," but at least it is real.

The poem's use of Africa is not an indictment of that continent or of the poet's African ancestry. Rather, it is a lamentation over how little of its memory survives in the present. In Cullen's poem, Africa endures as metaphor; it has been charged with "meaning but not memory."[5] Africa the concept has shaped the poet's identity, but Africa the continent is absent. Innocent of its colonial past or a political present, representing desires necessarily repressed and a question without an answer, Africa signifies both authenticity and its impossibility.

This poem could be read as autobiography; Cullen's family life lacked definition and stability. His biological father disappeared after his birth, and he was raised by his paternal grandmother until she passed away and he was adopted by her pastor. Despite regularly sending money to his mother, he remained estranged from her until his death. In this sense, Countee Cullen's literal "heritage" was unsettled, a source of unease for the young man wanting self-definition.[6]

The poem can also be read as a sort of auto-ethnography, a description not just of Cullen's heritage but also of a situation, a cultural location common to him and to others of African descent living in diaspora, estranged from their past by the practices of white supremacy, enduring a context hostile to collective self-definition. It is in this second sense that the poem makes a claim on public attention, enters public debate, and can exert an influence on belief and behavior. Thus this poem, though ostensibly one man's deeply personal exploration of his own identity, can also be read rhetorically, as an attempted transformation of shared meaning, an expression of a social truth that defines and has the potential to mobilize a population.[7] Read in this way, Cullen's poem is a strategic interpretation of raced experience in the context of the African Diaspora and an effort to make that interpretation a shared and compelling one.

This kind of rhetorical behavior has a long and varied history in the "New World," and it raises a number of questions about rhetorical history.[8] First, how has rhetoric that argues for a relationship between Africans in diaspora and Africa interacted with other discourses that have structured the expression of collective identity within modernity, specifically colonialism and nationalism? Second, how does diaspora function as a location from which arguments can enter the public sphere; how does rhetoric that articulates the interests of a population not defined by the boundaries of a state motivate collective action and influence policies?

This book pursues these questions through the analysis of a pivotal moment in the development of this discursive tradition, the 1930s. Specifically, it studies how colonialism shaped perceptions of Africa and its diaspora and, in turn, how that understanding influenced the manner in which people of African descent participated in public debate. In the following pages, I argue that during the 1930s the African Diaspora was transformed and reconstituted in black American rhetorical culture.

Prior to this period, many people of African descent had argued that Africa was a source of cultural and spiritual resources that would become perfect in the "New World." According to this narrative, black people in diaspora and Africans shared an ideal history; nevertheless, significant differences separated black people in the African Diaspora from each other and from Africa, generally prohibiting a common collective identity. After the 1920s, the meaning of Africa and the African Diaspora began to change, and people of African descent expressed new relationships among themselves, the United States, and the African Diaspora. Increasingly, black people began to interpret political crises involving people of color as evidence of a collusion of colonialism and racism and a coherence of ideology and policy.

During the U.S. occupation of Haiti, black newspapers and periodicals interpreted the massacre of unarmed Haitians by marines as evidence that racialized violence existed at a global level. Departing from the existential foundations that had characterized previous expressions of the African Diaspora, this rhetoric interpreted the circumstances facing that diaspora from a political perspective. Not only did this political framework create new opportunities for realizing an Afro-Diasporic community, it suggested a new collective identity for black Americans — a collective identity that included the African Diaspora as well as Africans. For example, George Schuyler's interpretation of the predicament of Liberian labor in the crisis of 1931 suggested that Afro-Diasporic community involved more than just the recognition of a shared geographic origin in Africa, it evolved from the synthesis of two political conditions, race and class, which existed around the globe. This growing sense of the African Diaspora as a coherent *political* identity culminated in the rhetoric of black Americans as they responded to the Italian invasion of Ethiopia in 1935. Rhetoric like that of J. A. Rogers expressed a truly mass, Afro-Diasporic political consciousness that did not require a negation of existential difference. I conclude that these new expressions of the Afro-Diasporic community reconfigured the scope and style of black American participation in U.S. democracy; it suggested rhetorical strategies for progressive politics and intervened in the logic of white supremacy with progressive visions of black identity. This book analyzes the historical context of this discursive evolution, the rhetoric through which this transformation occurred, and the contours of its political legacy.

A Rhetoric of Diaspora

Throughout the nineteenth century distant geographical spaces figured in rhetoric about and from people of African descent. Pro-slavery speakers often justified slavery's oppressive practice and legacy by associating a racist indictment of Africa and the African Diaspora with the character of Africans in the New World.[9]

People of African descent countered this discourse by referring to the African Diaspora in order to motivate domestic political agitation against white supremacy. The Haitian Revolution from 1791 to 1801 was one such bilingual event, providing both a rationale for repressive policies against blacks and a reservoir for progressive discourse.[10] European America was frightened by the events in Haiti and their implications for the domestic practice of slavery. Partly motivated by the Haitian revolution, the state of North Carolina established a two-year moratorium on the slave trade in 1792, and the federal government enacted the first national fugitive slave act in 1793. Although cessation of the slave trade may appear to have been progressive to contemporary sensibilities, in this context, it isolated and immobilized Africans in America.

Increased legal and social repression inspired by the Haitian revolution figured prominently in abolitionist rhetoric. Progressive European and African Americans in the nineteenth century used the African Diaspora as a model for black America's potential. David Walker obliquely referenced Haiti and the Caribbean in his 1829 "Appeal," arguing that "the inhabitants of the islands of the sea . . . are called men"[11]; and in his 1859 "Address to the Free People of Color of the State of Maryland," John Hall argued that on his first visit to Haiti "he first saw the black man administering government, and performing all functions properly appertaining to manhood."[12] For these two individuals, the heroes of the Haitian Revolution symbolized what African America could become.[13]

People of African descent also interpreted domestic events as relevant to the political condition of nations in the Diaspora. Black preachers like Peter J. Williams used Psalm 68:13 and its prophecy "And Ethiopia shall stretch forth her hands unto God" as a resource for moral argument, a lens through which to view domestic inequity, and a window into the imminence and character of emancipation. However, in his 1808 "Oration on the Abolition of the Slave Trade" Williams interpreted domestic political reform and the end of the slave trade as proof of Ethiopia's impending religious redemption and the consequent political redemption of both African America and the continent of Africa. In this discourse, the end of the slave trade was one step in a redemptive narrative that would be followed by emancipation, the civilization of Africa, and the transformation of Africa into U.S. middle-class Christianity.[14]

This broad sketch intimates how events within the African Diaspora influenced racial politics in the United States and black rhetorical culture. Characterizations of the African Diaspora justified repressive legislation, motivated progressive activism, and reflected domestic political conditions; in short, the African Diaspora itself has been defined in various ways, and these meanings have emerged through interactions between African, African American, and European American influences that are embedded in various political contexts and have served specific functions in those contexts.[15] This rhetoric of and about the African Diaspora is a corollary to the historical dispersion of African peoples.

The history of this rhetoric of the African Diaspora has been studied exhaustively and through a number of vocabularies, although each term entails its own theoretical assumptions and commitments. Afrocentricity, pan-Africanism, Black Nationalism, African Nationalism, the African Personality, and St. Clair Drake's "Africa Interest" are just a few of the theoretical terminologies employed to understand this phenomenon and its history.[16] Some of the scholarship that studies this history dismissively disarticulates the African Diaspora, like Stephen Howe's claim that Afrocentricity is essentially irrational due to the cultural and geographic distances between people of African descent.[17] Others, like Paul Gilroy, study the theoretical and philosophical implications of how travel by intellectuals of African descent created a coherent diaspora.[18] Recently, critics have begun to attend more carefully to the textual practices that constitute and complicate diasporic community. Brent Hayes Edwards coined the phrase the "Practice of Diaspora" to focus attention on how the circulation and translation of texts can create connections between dispersed peoples of African descent.[19] Another important contribution of Edwards's work is that it explores the roles that mistranslation and disjunction can play in shaping international community. His focus on how actual language practices create connections among people in diaspora is an important counterpoint to more literal or theoretical approaches to diaspora, but, as Michael Hanchard argues, Edwards's literary approach deemphasizes the political implications of these textual practices.[20]

While scholars who study rhetoric typically are positioned at this nexus between public expression and politics, the business of rhetorical study admits diverse definitions of rhetoric. Some scholars focus exclusively on oratory or the instruments of persuasion; others attend to the politics of discourse more generally. The perspective on rhetoric taken in this book, as I explain below, bridges these approaches by focusing on how rhetoric creates collective identities and positions those identities to act politically.

A rhetorical approach to diaspora assumes that the contours and scope of the African Diaspora, specifically the relative intimacy between its communities and their logics of association, are all constituted in public expressions. Diaspora is a communicative event and a strategic interpretation of trans-state community. Thus, although the term "diaspora" suggests a community defined by its dislocation from a geographic center (thus excluding Africans still inside Africa from the African Diaspora), a particular rhetoric that constitutes the diaspora may include those who have not been "dispersed." That is, the rhetorical community of diaspora may include Africans — or it may not. The point is that, from a rhetorical perspective, international black community, like all political community, is shaped through the "constitutive" function of public arguments that I shall examine in this book.

In 1950 Kenneth Burke turned from "persuasion" to "identification" as a master trope for explaining human intercourse through language and thus initiated a shift in the priorities of rhetorical critics. Burke claimed that rhetorical exchange is more than an agency for accomplishing persuasive goals. He inspired rhetorical critics to explore rhetoric's ontological dimensions, its capacity to create reality. Moreover, after Burke, rhetorical critics interrogated "audience" through this frame; that is, they understood audience, not as a natural or given element in rhetorical exchange, but as a reality created by discourse.[21]

Michael Calvin McGee cited Burke as an inspiration for his highly influential 1975 article, "In Search of the People: A Rhetorical Alternative." McGee claimed that rhetorical critics had misunderstood Burke's thought and its implications for theorizing audience. According to McGee, conventional critics deemphasized the impact that Hegel, Marx, and Freud had had on Burke's thought. Consequently, they neglected Burke's insight into the character of human collective behavior; they assumed that audiences preceded discourse and that groups of people behaved as an ideal individual would. That is to say, they assumed that groups of people could be understood as individuals writ large.[22] Departing from the view of these scholars, McGee contended that collectivities are complicated and the result of rhetorical practices. He argued that "'the people' are more process than phenomenon" and that "a kind of rhetoric defines 'the people' at each stage in a 'collectivization process' of coming to be an objectively real entity."[23] These rhetorical processes take the form of particular political myths that organize collective belief into an identity. Accordingly, McGee argued, critics should attend to those rhetorical practices which propose "a new rhetoric, a new mythology"—in short, a new identity.[24]

Following Burke and McGee, Maurice Charland investigated the articulation of one such political mythology, the "White Paper" published by the Parti Quebecois in 1979, and in the course of this work he coined a term to explain rhetoric's relationship to identity, "constitutive rhetoric."[25] Charland argues that subjectivity is ontologically prior to persuasion, because "one must already be an interpellated subject and exist as a discursive position in order to be part of the audience of a rhetorical situation in which persuasion could occur."[26] In Charland's analysis, the "White Paper" created a "national identity for a new type of political subject."[27] Rhetoric's power, Charland contends, is in this ability to create identities situated to enter public discourse and act politically.

Despite constitutive rhetoric's attention to textual expressions of group identity, it fails to appreciate the rhetorical behavior of real people. Constitutive rhetoric explores what sociologists call social identity, or the public roles that individuals are invited to play.[28] Thus the subject of constitutive rhetoric is an ideological effect—an ideal—and, in many ways, it is as reductive as the monolithic sense of audience that McGee sets out to refute. Constitutive rhetoric underemphasizes the processes through which interested individuals form collectivities. A corollary tradition in sociology, New Social Movement theory, provides a counterpoint to the scholarship of constitutive rhetoric through the vocabulary of "collective identity."[29]

Sociologists working within the New Social Movement paradigm contend that a new kind of collective political behavior has emerged in postmodernity. Prior social movement activity was animated by class membership and the material interests of an oppressed class; these social movements agitated in traditional political forums for specific policies and the redistribution of resources. In contrast, since the 1960s new social movements have cut across class lines, focused on lifestyle issues, and worked for social change through quotidian cultural performances.[30] The historical argument here is not compelling, but New Social Movement theory does explain how "identity" is actually both a goal for political action and an effect of coordinated behaviors rather than a preexisting condition. Social Movement theorist Alberto Melucci defines this activity of "collective identity" as an "interactive and shared definition produced by several individuals (or groups at a more complex level) and concerned with the orientations of action and the field of opportunities and constraints in which the action takes place."[31] As a "shared definition," collective identity establishes a context in which individuals recognize "common cognitive frameworks that enable them to assess their environment and to calculate the costs and benefits of their action."[32]

As rhetoric shapes populations it also provides a foundation from which individuals can speak. Thus, a rhetorical approach to diaspora implies attention to how "diaspora" can itself serve as a space from which an argument can enter public debate.[33] At particular moments, within particular controversies, the collective identity of diaspora has been evoked with particular effects on popular beliefs and public policies. Rhetorical critics in the field of communication studies often study rhetorical efficacy as the aftereffect of a text and neglect the place from which the text emanated, namely the necessarily contingent and constructed cultural position of the speaking subject. Lack of attention to this detail is understandable. Clearly, political discourse tends to be more effective when it comes from a citizen of the nation-state concerned. Within this framework, however, state boundaries are assumed rather than created or given meaning, thus circumscribing the potential to understand how discourse and politics shape and bridge borders.

For example, Martin Medhurst has called for scholarship more international in scope, advising critics to study rhetorical practices performed in languages other than English.[34] Although he argues for criticism across borders—learning Spanish, for example, and studying Mexican discourse—he makes no provision for the study of discourse that may exist between and within national boundaries as defined by state structures. Although couched in a language that argues for a more global perspective, his suggestion remains wedded to a logic of nations as coextensive with political borders. In a similar fashion, Dexter Gordon's excellent study of the rhetoric of Black Nationalism in the nineteenth century attends to the creation of the rhetorical subject but neglects to consider how the black-speaking subject of the nineteenth century was, to a large degree, produced by cultural and political forces not circumscribed by the borders of the United States.[35] As Amritjit Singh and Peter Schmidt argue in their introduction to *Postcolonial Theory and the United States: Race, Ethnicity, and Literature,* a presupposed state framework neglects the discursive creation of borders, the global dimensions of identity construction, and hybridity as basic forms in identity construction and expressive traditions.[36]

Recently this critical, post-national stance has turned up in literary studies and U.S. studies in the form of an approach called hemisphereism, which entails excavation of the "intricate and complex politics, histories, and discourses of spatial encounter that have generally been obscured in U.S. nation-based inquiries."[37] Scholarship within this tradition "triangulates" U.S. history and attempts to displace dichotomies of black/white or foreign/domestic in favor of directing critical attention to how the "American" came to be. Michelle Stephens explains that such an approach is characterized by treatment of transatlantic history as "layered, multiracial, and multinational."[38] By adopting a post-national, hemispheric approach to rhetoric in this book, I look at how discourses and texts that travel across the borders of a state can complicate the normative authority of the state-bound citizen as speaking subject and explore the political potential of rhetoric that emerges from this position. Ultimately, the rhetoric of diaspora and the texts under consideration here are efforts to craft a new space from which people of African descent can speak with influence.

The rhetorical position that is the object of this book — that is, the collective identity of a "citizen" of the African Diaspora — is inextricably linked to discourses of modernity and cosmopolitanism; after all, within European modernity the cosmopolitan is the paradigmatic actor across state borders, and the modern state was, both literally and figuratively, built on the back of raced labor. Equally important, as Michael Hanchard argues, is the fact that progressive black political activity, from Black Nationalism to the modern civil rights movement, is "undergirded" by response to "some notion of practice of modernity." For example, activists within social and cultural movements that have endeavored to end the political subordination of people of African descent have employed particularly modern understandings of citizenship and political community while responding to exclusion from these categories. Afro-modern politics employ transnational networks to critique the uneven application of the "discourses of the Enlightenment" and the asymmetrical practices of modernization, networks themselves made possible by the seismic cultural shifts and technological innovations that gave birth to modernity. Thus, as Hanchard explains, Afro-modern politics are "more than just responses to the Middle Passage and racial slavery. They are responses to the age and the technological, normative, and societal conditions that made the Middle Passage and racial slavery possible."[39]

Despite this central role played by modernity in progressive black politics, as Sibylle Fischer demonstrates through her analysis of radical abolitionism in the Caribbean, the relationship between modernity and the African Diaspora has been repressed.[40] The Haitian revolution, for example, despite embodying many of the fundamental precepts of the Enlightenment, signifies more as an absence or specter than as a constitutive event in historical narratives of modernity. Following Fischer, Ifeoma Kiddoe Nwankwo demonstrates how the resources of modernity were differentially configured for populations of the African Diaspora during the nineteenth century.[41] Her study of abolitionism in the rhetorics of Cuban poet Placido and Frederick Douglass demonstrates that the cosmopolitan modern was not a space from which racially progressive black rhetoric could have significant political impact during the nineteenth century. These two fine studies document how rhetoric that invoked modernity and inspired progressive black international community struggled to impact public policies and make a difference in the reality of raced experience in the nineteenth century.

Two recent books study this rhetoric of diaspora and Afro-modern politics as they enter the twentieth century. The first, *Race against Empire* by Penny Von Eschen, is an excellent study that documents the political work of international black activists like W. E. B. Du Bois and Paul Robeson in the context of the emerging Cold War. The second, *Proudly We Can be Africans* by James Meriweather, studies the development of black anticolonial consciousness in the United States and Africa from the Italian invasion of Ethiopia to decolonization in Africa and the 1960s. Both of these books treat black activism in response to the Italian invasion of Ethiopia as a beginning—the origin of the anticolonial consciousness that would eventually challenge colonial oppression in Africa and in the United States—but neither attends carefully to the role of public expression in creating this consciousness or to the historical and rhetorical events that laid the foundation for this iteration of black activism.

To explore these issues fully this book is divided into two parts. The first section outlines the theoretical and historical issues at stake in this project and frames the criticism that follows within conversations about colonialism and black history. The second section is a series of case studies of African American anticolonial discourse. I close with an interpretation of the significance of the discourse under study in both its immediate and its future contexts.

In chapter 1, I discuss the emergence of colonialism as a coherent discourse and set of rhetorical and political practices. Colonialism was a phase in the Western practice of imperialism during which state power perpetuated asymmetrical trading relationships between industrial and preindustrial states. These relationships were maintained through cultural leadership and the imposition of distinct spheres of labor in colonized and colonizing populations. Colonial ideology assumed that colonialism was a natural and beneficial process through which the civilization of a European core would be diffused to a colonized periphery.

Chapter 2 explores the role of diffusionist assumptions in the expression of black ethos. The principle of diffusion structured the modern nation; consequently, black Americans employed and configured the rhetoric of diffusionism as they expressed the character of black America. In the early years of the twentieth century this rhetoric focused on Africa. The continent and its cultures became the central element of a new rhetoric that expressed an international black ethos, a vision of black character acting in a global context. I explore these interlocking issues—diffusionism, "Africa," and black ethos—through the analysis of the Pan-African rhetoric of W. E. B. Du Bois and Marcus Garvey. Du Bois and Garvey argued that Africa was central to black experience. Through their public pronouncements about Africa, they tried to craft a new "sense of place" for black people; they argued that black identity was performed in an international arena and shifted the circumference of black experience away from the political borders created by white supremacy. Despite this progressive stance, they also reproduced the diffusionist assumptions of contemporaneous nationalisms; both assumed a linear, asymmetrical mode of commerce between pure, core, and peripheral cultural spaces intranationally (between black social classes) and internationally (between new and old world Africans). Ultimately, for Du Bois and Garvey, I argue that Africa was an existential resource, and black ethos, the context in which black character was formed, was metaphysical, a ground of coordinate essences rather than shared political conditions. The next three chapters discuss the shift from this existentially based paradigm to one that engaged contemporary Africa on more political and reciprocal terms.

In chapter 3, I investigate African American responses to the U. S. occupation of Haiti. In 1915, citing a need to protect democracy and the stability of the Caribbean, the United States invaded Haiti. By 1920 Haitian military resistance had been suppressed and the occupation was mostly bureaucratic. The invasion and occupation became pressing concerns in black American discourse in the late 1920s. In 1929, at the Haitian port of Aux Cayes, U.S. marines fired on a group of unarmed Haitians who were protesting the occupation. Responding to the violence at Aux Cayes, black Americans expressed an innovative articulation of the African Diaspora. In newspapers and periodicals, the crisis at Aux Cayes was seen as colonial and racially violent. I conclude that the interpretation of the Africa Diaspora that emerged from the U.S. occupation of Haiti performed a new, significant function in the rhetoric of black America. Departing from the existential function served by previous interpretations, black American newspapers articulated a meaning for the African Diaspora that was based on a political framework. Still, despite a newly perceived political intimacy between black Americans and the Diaspora, the rhetoric of black newspapers and periodicals in the United States did not escape a diffusionist paternalism toward mass Haitian culture.

Chapter 4 suggests how the political interpretation of the African Diaspora that began with the crisis in Haiti made possible a further imagination of diasporic collective identity through the coordination of political conditions, in particular the correlation of race and class. I locate the development of this rhetoric in African American responses to the Liberian labor crisis of 1926–1932. As the 1920s drew to a close, the labor policies of the Americo-Liberian government came under international scrutiny. A 1927 trade agreement with the Firestone Corporation gave the company control over many of the country's resources, most notably its native labor force. In 1929 the U.S. chargé d'affaires issued a rebuke that characterized Liberian labor practices as "hardly distinguishable from organized slave trade."[42] Prominent black intellectuals like W. E. B. Du Bois and Alain Locke defended the Liberian government, suggesting that it too had been dominated by the power of Western capital and bullied into labor practices that, although unfortunate, were distinct from U.S. chattel slavery in meaningful ways.[43]

George Schuyler disagreed with this dissociation of African and American histories of exploitation. His 1931 novel *Slaves Today: A Story of Liberia* illustrated how black workers around the globe were forced to endure the dehumanizing bureaucracies of the bourgeoisie and the obtrusion of racial thinking into their daily lives, both of which created static cultural spaces that denied the progressive potential of modernity. I conclude that the subject who thrives in the liminal spaces of race and class comes to define how black Americans increasingly viewed themselves and the African Diaspora. I conclude, as well, that this constituted identity represents the growing sympathy of black Americans for people of African descent who experienced a matrix of racial oppression that was global in its scope.

In chapter 5, I discuss African American responses to the Italian invasion of Ethiopia in 1935. As Italy prepared to invade Ethiopia, black America rallied to its defense through public protest and political organization. Response was especially passionate in urban centers like Chicago and Harlem, where a special political culture facilitated the creation of a self-referential field of knowledge about the African Diaspora. Joel A. Rogers's pamphlet "The Real Facts about Ethiopia" exemplifies the Afro-Diasporic consciousness that circulated in this context. I argue that Rogers's text critiques the nature of race under colonialism by illustrating how state boundaries and racial categories are coordinate, arbitrary operations of colonial power. In contrast, the text represents Ethiopia as heterogeneous and borderless. I conclude that this image of Ethiopia created a temporal frame for overcoming the diffusionist logic of colonialism; it constituted an extracolonial memory of Afro-Diasporic consciousness founded in present, everyday experiences with white supremacy.

In the concluding chapter I discuss the historical and theoretical significance of the rhetorical shift I observed in the critical case studies. The themes that emerged during the 1930s persisted in subsequent political and cultural action. Black anticolonialism in the 1930s was expressed through a coherent rhetoric that provided a vocabulary for antiracist movements throughout the twentieth century.

CHAPTER I

The Politics and Practices
of Colonialism

BLACK ANTICOLONIAL RHETORIC emerged in the context of America's history with colonialism. What "colonialism" was (is) and America's relationship to it are issues of public and scholarly debate today. This chapter explores colonialism from both historical and theoretical perspectives in a search to understand the implications of colonialist discourse for domestic rhetorical cultures. My purpose is to provide an operational definition of colonialism and a historical and political context for the emergence of colonial practices not only relative to the United States but also in the broader frameworks of imperialism and empire.

Contemporary scholars of discourse study colonialism primarily through the abstract and often decontextualed notion of the "postcolonial." Postcolonial studies of literature have paid considerable attention to the development of subjectivity in the context of imperialism, but the historical, political, and cultural dimensions of colonialism have received less scholarly scrutiny.[1] Abdul JanMohamed argues that this scholarly focus on the textual and psychological dimensions of postcoloniality has deemphasized the historical realities of colonialism and the asymmetry of colonial power in practice. He suggests a more contextual approach to the dynamics of colonialism, arguing that we "can better understand colonialist discourse . . . through analysis that maps its ideological function in relation to actual imperialist practices."[2] R. Radhakrishnan argues that studies of colonialism and postcoloniality have fetishized postcolonial deterritorialization through theoretical categories like "diaspora" while paying little attention to the actual practices of colonialism

15

or the meaning of diaspora. This aestheticization of a particular kind of "difference," Radhakrishnan asserts, is "completely at odds with the actual experience of difference as undergone by diasporic peoples."[3] Rather than relying on atemporal and often abstract theoretical constructs of identity, a more useful understanding of colonialism and its legacy may be possible through the study of historically specific political and rhetorical practices.

There are several benefits to be gained from following the advice of these scholars. First, attention to the historical and political dimensions of colonialism respects the complexity and variety of experiences within that system and their articulation over time. Second, this critical approach complicates postcolonial theory by encouraging scholars to attend to the dynamics of a particular colonial moment. For example, much postcolonial theory is derived from the close textual analysis of literature; however, one might legitimately question whether the political economy of literature's production leaves room for the full texture of colonial experience, especially among a populace that may have to struggle just to obtain the basic necessities of everyday life. The study of colonialism in the Great Depression, for example, would be inadequate if one did not investigate a variety of texts, genres, and media that held cultural and political authority at the time. In this sense, a historically grounded approach to colonialism extends the field of discursive practices that interpret colonial experience beyond the realm of the bourgeois intellectual. In order better to understand what colonialism is and its relationship to U.S. racial politics, this chapter explores the historical emergence of colonialism, investigates the political and ideological practices that constitute colonial power, and speculates about how colonialism has influenced black rhetorical culture.

Imperialism and the Emergence of Colonialism

Scholars in diverse fields have debated the temporal parameters of the "colonial"; some suggest that colonialism began in 1492 and continues today, while others argue for the necessity to draw a distinction between imperialism as a general attitude of European expansion and colonialism as a specific economic and political practice.[4] Patrick Williams and Laura Chrisman persuasively argue that imperialism refers to the extension of capitalist modes of production to precapitalist regions of the globe and that colonialism refers to a historical moment when the importance of state power to this process increased, causing a period of European "conquest and direct control of other people's land."[5] In this sense, the modern economic and political project of colonialism was both a period and a set of practices in the ongoing processes of Western imperialism.

From this perspective, a perspective I adopt, the larger project of Western imperialism began in the sixteenth century with the marked increase in European exploitation of resources across the globe. Technological innovations in shipbuilding, astronomy, and cartography created greater intimacy between Europe and the Americas, Asia, and Africa, and accelerated the diffusion and counterdiffusion of a wide spectrum of cultural influences and material goods.[6] These advancements were complemented by developments in public media that facilitated the extension of imperial power and the establishment of asymmetrical trading relationships.[7] Most important, however, this process influenced culture, politics, and the economy in both the "new" world and the "old."[8] At the close of the eighteenth century, increased contact between Europe and the Americas, Asia, and Africa coincided with Enlightenment assumptions about the power of reason and emerging conceptions of culture and nationality.

Early naturalists who considered cultural difference played an important role in the ideology that guided imperialist practice. For example, Johann Friedrich Blumenbach, inspired by "exotic" populations, distinguished races of mankind and their relative capabilities. According to him, geography and culture ordained innate differences between communities of human beings. He retained faith in the biblical narrative of the singular, Adamic origin of humankind but argued that climate, culture, and living conditions produced distinct races with particular intellectual capacities. Although Blumenbach's evaluation of non-European cultures was decidedly pejorative, nonetheless its assumptions suggested the potential for cultural change and intellectual development in African, Asian, and American populations.[9]

German cultural theorist Johan Herder perceived differences among European, American, Asian, and African cultures in a similar vein.[10] Presaging the arguments of twentieth-century anthropology, he argued for a kind of cultural relativism. He suggested that cultures were composed of a communal consciousnesses expressed in folk traditions. Moreover, cultures had distinct natures and destinies. In pursuing its destiny, every culture could fulfill the ultimate purpose of humankind as ordained by

God. Although Herder was critical of European expansionist tendencies and popular assumptions about Africa, Asia, and the Americas, his work was used to justify both separate racial and cultural spheres and an imperative for European domination of globe, seen as the particular destiny of European nations.[11]

Blumenbach and Herder represent a much larger European intellectual effort to understand a rapidly changing political and cultural landscape at the close of the eighteenth century. As Edward Said documents in *Orientalism*, at the onset of the nineteenth century, theories of race and culture inspired European governments and industries to increase their involvement in the generation of knowledge about the foreign spaces on which they relied. Explorers, subsidized by European political and economic interests, traveled to Africa and Asia and throughout the Americas with two interrelated goals: to create economic opportunities for the sponsoring state and to accumulate knowledge that could be used to further enhance the aims of capital. Said discusses this particular expression of power and knowledge through Napoleon's twenty-year study of Egypt. In 1798 Napoleon brought a team of scholars with him on his expedition to Egypt. These scholars studied Egyptian culture and geography and, from 1809 to 1828, published their findings in a nineteen-volume series entitled *Description de L'Egypte*. The study purported to understand Egypt and Egyptian culture in its entirety. According to Said, Napoleon's study was a watershed in the history of Western imperialism; it was the first state-commissioned ethnographic study of such magnitude and comprehensiveness.[12]

Napoleon's study allowed French scholars to act as agents of the state and to further articulate the bourgeois intellectual class to state power. Furthermore, the study and its putative objectivity transmuted Egyptian "cultural" difference into "racial" difference by removing Egyptian cultural practices from their natural contexts and fixing them as subordinate within a Western narrative of civilization. Within this register, cultural particularity acquired both permanence and a moral valence; it signified "difference" as an "otherness" against which European moral and social excellence was measured. In this sense, the modern notion of race is inextricable from both colonialism and bourgeois intellectual labor. Napoleon's study is just one well-known example of a rhetorical practice that was widespread in the nineteenth century.[13]

These political and intellectual developments had a corollary in popular culture. For example, Jean François Champolion's 1822 deciphering of the Rosetta Stone made the study of distant cultures a prominent issue in Europe and in the United States' nascent popular culture. Concurrently, the British Museum began acquiring Asian sculptures. These statues and obelisks were displayed in prominent public spaces in London. Thus, at the onset of the nineteenth century, Europe placed knowledge about Asia, Africa, and the Americas in a matrix of state interest and popular appetite.[14]

These intellectual and cultural trends evolved concomitantly with the politics of Western imperialism and fueled the emergence of the modern nation. European culture developed a posture toward the cultures of Asia, Africa, and the Americas, an attitude toward geography and cultural development, and a relationship between knowledge and power that isolated an identifiable "other" and articulated an imperative for engagement. At the close of the nineteenth century the logic of imperialism inspired and legitimated Western intervention in non-Western culture, economics, politics, and religion; indeed, the very identity of Western civilization was inextricably linked to a particular knowledge of Africa and Asia that was sustained through an epistemology of imperial control and the circulation of capital from Western to non-Western shores and then back again.

Practices of Colonial Power

Two conferences of European leaders in the second half of the nineteenth century refined the processes of imperialism and explicitly linked that project to state policies. In 1876 King Leopold of Belgium invited several dozen explorers to Brussels for a conference about Africa. In his opening remarks, Leopold announced his agenda to "open to civilization the only part of the globe which it has not yet penetrated, to pierce the darkness which hangs over entire peoples."[15] The conference resulted in the formation of the International African Association to promote the study and exploitation of Africa.[16] Years later, German chancellor Otto von Bismarck convened the Berlin West African Conference. The European powers, the United States, and the Ottoman Empire met to carve up Africa while limiting the potential for competing claims and violent conflict. The conference led to rules that governed Europe's acquisition of African territory;

for example, governments and their agents were required to inform other state powers of their intent to possess a territory and to validate possession with occupation. These two conferences rapidly changed the pace of African colonization. In 1880, approximately 80 percent of Africa was ruled by Africans, but in less than twenty years nearly all of Africa was occupied by European states.[17]

Colonial occupation took several forms; in Africa, Britain established white settler colonies (Kenya and Zimbabwe), indirect-rule colonies (Nigeria and Botswana), and direct-rule colonies (Senegal). Each form of colonial control necessitated distinct investments from the British and native Africans and had particular consequences for African cultures as well as for the culture of the occupiers. White settler colonies, for example, established elite caste systems and new traditions like the "gentleman farmer" identity for lower-class immigrants in order to promote self-esteem and respect. Because the form of colonization differed from place to place, the degree of European investment also differed. Some colonies were limited to small numbers of European administrators, traders, and missionaries. In northern Nigeria, there was one white administrator for every hundred thousand Africans. Approximately 5 percent of Africans were educated in Western missionary schools, and this minority assumed supporting positions in the colonial system.[18] This system of education sped the development of a middle class that profited from colonialism and contributed to the exploitation of the colonized majority.

In addition, colonialism created a circulation of capital that benefited Europe while it simultaneously inhibited the development of indigenous economies. The controlling state used its initial investment of men and material to export raw goods and labor to the West. It then converted these resources into manufactured products and exported the products back to "developing" countries through exploitative trade arrangements. In this very material circulation of capital, African markets were flooded with cheap mass-produced textile, glass and iron products, consequently undermining the indigenous community's ability to manufacture the same products.[19]

At the beginning of the twentieth century, Liberia and Ethiopia were the only African countries not occupied by European power. Despite its independence, Liberia was beholden to European states and banking interests through a series of usurious loans initiated in the 1870s, and Ethiopia maintained its autonomy only by repelling an attempted colonial incursion by Italy in 1896 and castrating fifteen hundred Italian prisoners of war before releasing them from capture.[20]

The colonization of Africa was one arena of Western imperial expansion that reached its apex during the period from the 1880s to the outbreak of World War I; concurrent European and U.S. colonial efforts were made in Asia and in the Caribbean. Analysis of this colonial moment and other European colonial projects has enabled scholars to identify a number of general characteristics of colonialism.

Political, Cultural, and Ideological Implications of Colonialism

Fred Lee Hord, in his study *Reconstructing Memory: Black Literary Criticism,* distills the work of postcolonial theorists Amilcar Cabral, Frantz Fanon, and Alberto Memmi to suggest three basic characteristics of colonial policy.[21] Hord argues that colonialism is fundamentally concerned with the disposition of goods and the enrichment of the West. Thus, colonialism is material; its motor is greed and its mode is violent. Equally important, however, is the fact that colonialism manipulates the culture of the colonized in order to achieve its material ends. Often outnumbered and far from their homeland, colonial governments were maintained only by "the permanent, organized repression of cultural life of the people concerned."[22] Last, representatives of the colonial state administer these political and cultural policies; colonial bureaucracies enforce population-specific legislation that disciplines the colonized populations and configures economic and social opportunity.

These three practices — material exploitation, cultural transformation, and bureaucratic administration — form the core of colonial governance and create cultures of colonialism. In *Still the Big News: Racial Oppression in America,* Bob Blauner describes the culture of the colonized by considering the similarities and differences of the colonial condition in relation to the experiences of the immigrant.[23] He argues that the colonial condition consists of four basic elements. First, colonial populations endure a forced relationship with the colonial power; they are either living in occupied space or suffer the jurisdiction of the colonizer because of forced movement.

Second, as is suggested by the political practices described above, indigenous elements of colonial culture are undermined by the colonial system; colonial bureaucracies disrupt the cultural practices and folk lives of colonized communities. This disruption contributes to the third characteristic of the colonial condition, an ambiguous relationship between colonial bureaucracy and colonized populations. Colonial agents live in close proximity with those populations, and each assumes characteristics of the other, highlighting the hybridity of identity and creating tension between authentic and "compromised" cultural identifications.[24]

Last, despite the hybridity just mentioned, the colonial condition is characterized by racism. Colonialism articulates static, putatively inherent racial identities as the foundation of rigid social hierarchies. In this sense, although colonialism is characterized by increased intimacy between the West and Asia and Africa, its political and cultural dynamics strive to differentiate those two populations. From Blauner's perspective, these elements of colonialism evident in the histories of Asia and Africa also apply to the United States. Africans in U.S. chattel slavery and in their occupied homelands endured a similarly involuntary association with Western power, a disruption of their cultural heritage, a confusion of their identity, and a process of racist othering.

Colonialism, Identity, and Cultural Diffusion

The colonial contest has deep implications for how individuals understand and perform identity. Homi Bhabha argues that colonialism demonstrates the impossibility of retaining essential identity or autonomous culture. All identity and all cultural traditions are constituted in the linguistic possibilities through which a self and an "other" acquire meaning. Bhabha discusses colonialism through the frame of subjectivity and the "third space" in which cultures and subjectivities form.[25]

The theoretical problems of culture and identity encountered within colonial settings have two implications that are especially germane to this study. First, all identity is hybrid, because individual and cultural identity is negotiated: it is relational and never independent. Thus, in a colonial context, "colonized" and "colonizing" identities and cultures are coextensive; colonized and colonizing cultures are articulated both in colonialism and in each other. Second, Bhabha shifts the terrain of culture from the temporal to the spatial. A negotiated, relational identity is impossible to fix in time or history because it is constantly shifting. In this sense, identity becomes a function of proximity; it evolves in and through the manipulation of discursive spaces. Fundamentally, then, colonialism manipulates the intimacy between putatively discrete populations, assuming, suggesting, and thereby creating distinctions and relations between intimate peoples and spaces. Most obviously, "space" matters, because Western and colonial populations originated in separate political spaces and regions of the globe; but the discrete cultural spaces shaped in Asia, Africa, and the Americas were equally important.

Cultural, political, and geographic spaces within colonialism were conceived as having one of two essential natures. A culture, a state, a region, could be the "core" or the "periphery," colonizer or colonized, or, more important, the source of progress and modernity or its beneficiary. Commerce between these spaces within colonialism, then, was regulated by an ideology that assumed a fertile core from which cultural and economic progress would emanate and influence the development of its static periphery. J. M. Blaut calls this ideology "Eurocentric Diffusionism."[26]

In the heyday of colonial expansion, cultural evolution often was explained in terms of internal or external development. Cultures were thought to change because of autonomous innovation or the influence of externalities like exposure to other cultures through war, missionary efforts, or cross-cultural commerce, for example. Each theory of culture, called "independent invention" and "diffusionism," respectively, relied upon certain assumptions about the nature of human society. Independent invention privileged the autonomy of a culture and the relative impermeability of its borders. Diffusionism, on the other hand, assumed that human societies were essentially imitative and that cultural transmission was unidirectional. According to the diffusionist paradigm, under colonialism, the Western core developed the static or empty colonial periphery; the West possessed historical agency while Asia, Africa, and the indigenous Americas imitated its example, developing economically, politically, and spiritually through association with Western cultures.

The exchange of goods and labor between Europe, the United States, and Asia, Africa, and the Americas paradoxically evidenced the unidirectional nature of cultural growth. The export of manufactured goods to colonial countries mirrored the transmission of refined social structures and spiritual concepts, and the raw materials that counter-diffused to Europe and the United States were compensation for the benefits of the colonial relationship. This counter-diffusion suggested that colonial relationships were voluntary and participatory, but they were fundamentally asymmetrical; cultural diffusion had more value than its material counterpart. Moreover, individuals also considered counter-diffusion from the periphery as the source of any number of diseases and maladies of the mind and body. Diffusion was a necessary and beneficial remaking of the world in the image of the core, but its converse provided the dangerous potential for ideological and physical corruption, decadence, and disease. The discourse of colonialism suggested a mutually beneficial, though fundamentally asymmetrical, relationship between discrete cultural spaces. The framework of diffusionism illustrates how the flow of goods and culture between the core or metropole and the colonial periphery became construed as beneficent, as a sacrifice that had to be made by the West in the name of human progress.

As we shall see, this diffusionist ideology influenced nationalist rhetorics and U.S. racial politics. White supremacist articulations of "American" culture, progressive visions of U.S. democratic culture, and radical Black Nationalist agendas posited cultural centers and peripheries, and much of their political authority was derived from demands to police or expand the borders of these cultural spaces. Moreover, the diffusion of civilization through imitation of the core culture has its own, complicated history in U.S. racial politics.[27]

Although the United States was not an active military presence in the "scramble for Africa," nor did it obtain colonial possessions in the same scope or manner as European powers, the country itself was the product of a colonial relationship and imposed colonial schemes in a domestic context. As Juan Carlos Rowe argues in *Colonialism and Literature,* the United States "developed techniques of colonization in the course of breaking the colonial rule of Great Britain and establishing its own national identity. Such colonial practices emphasized the control of different peoples, their labor, and their means of communal identification."[28] Thus, even though the United States appeared largely to abstain from wholesale indulgence in the colonial land grab, residue from the former colony's proximity to its colonial masters was manifest in domestic cultural politics. Throughout the nineteenth century European America delineated distinct populations, undermined Native American and African cultural traditions, and assumed a unidirectional "diffusionist" model of social progress. As might be expected, black America enjoys an ambiguous relationship with U.S. colonialism; black America has had to endure a colonial condition yet also has utilized the rhetorical resources of colonialism in its agitation for social change.

African America and Colonialism

As already suggested, domestic race relations emerged in tandem with colonial expansion. Many of the same arguments that forwarded European expansion supported U.S. imperialism in Asia and the Caribbean and influenced the character of U.S. policies toward Native American and African American populations. Viewing domestic racial politics in this international frame highlights how "the history of black America is an act in the larger drama of the worldwide colonization of peoples of color by Europeans."[29]

Some argue that African America cannot be understood in the language of colonialism; since black Americans are not technically indigenous to America they are not colonized in the classical sense. Still, since the slave trade ceased in 1808, by the middle of the nineteenth century an overwhelming majority of black America was born in the United States, and most African Americans were living within the boundaries of the only homeland they knew when they were subjected to the colonial policies of white supremacy. Therefore, despite apparent dissimilarities in the mechanisms of colonialism and domestic race oppression, "a common process of social oppression characterized the racial patterns in the two contexts."[30]

Further, the U.S. tradition of segregation and racially specific legislation demonstrates this symmetry between European colonialism and domestic racial politics. In the nineteenth century the free black middle class came into increasing contact with Euro-America. White America enacted legislation to distinguish the two populations and to regulate social commerce between black and white America. Throughout antebellum America, states as diverse as Georgia, Indiana, and Minnesota enacted legislation to limit the public presence of black Americans through race-specific behavioral restrictions (e.g., not allowing blacks to play musical instruments after sunset or to smoke a pipe in public), bars on interstate immigration, and segregated schools.[31]

Even organizations that ostensibly worked for black social and economic progress, such as the American Missionary Association and American Freedmen's Union Commission, did so by filling a perceived absence in black culture: proper moral development. These organizations and others like them believed that blacks had special needs due to their temperamental character and their spiritual and moral weaknesses. Thus, even progressive organizations that attempted to improve the conditions

under which blacks lived were saturated with a racist ideology that believed in different capacities and correspondingly different public spaces,
namely segregated schools.[32] Moreover, both segregationist and civili-
zationist programs aspired to isolating black populations, attempted to
diagnose black American moral capacity, and assumed that moral and
political excellence originated in Euro-American populations and could
be disseminated through imitation by black America. In the antebellum
era, black America was "segregated by law, disfranchised, robbed of its
share of wages by discriminatory employment patterns, confronted by a
police power and illegal mobs acting in the role of occupational force,
the target of a mass culture of racism and the barbarism of lynching" and
was thus "imprisoned in a colonial relationship, designed by the new industrial power elite of America, at the very time that European colonists
were partitioning the African continent among themselves."[33] In this
sense, black America has endured colonial politics and cultural practices.
Still, colonialism figures ambivalently in black American rhetorical history. The discourse of colonialism that justified racist domestic policies
was also manifest in many progressive black American portrayals of the
African Diaspora. Thus, the violence of colonialist practices and the progressive potential of the rhetorical resources of colonialist rhetoric exist in
tension in black American rhetorical culture.

Black Thought and Colonial Practice: The Example of Lott Cary

Black America's ambiguous relationship to the discourse and ideology of
colonialism is exemplified by the life and rhetorical career of nineteenth-
century activist Lott Cary, and a rhetorical examination of his public discourse reveals much about this relationship. Born a slave in Virginia, Cary
taught himself to read and was profoundly influenced by two books, the
Bible and Adam Smith's *The Wealth of Nations*.[34] He labored and saved
and eventually bought freedom for himself and his two children in 1815.
Despite this accomplishment and its implication that social status was
not completely static in the United States, Cary remained critical of U.S.
racial politics. In 1821 he wrote: "I am an African; and in this country,
however meritorious my conduct and respectable my character, I cannot
receive the credit due to either. I wish to go to a country where I shall be
esteemed by my merits—not by my complexion—and I feel bound to

labor for my suffering race."[35] In 1821 Cary emigrated to the west coast of Africa. From the area that would become Liberia in 1847, Cary engaged in public debates about African American participation in United States democracy. In a public letter sent in 1827 Cary argued that black Americans should immigrate to Africa, because only there could they achieve true political and moral agency.[36]

Cary's rhetoric rests upon characterizations of American and African spaces and how they relate to each other. He argues that African space is fundamentally different from that of the United States; Africa is free of the debilitating structures of prejudice and politics that inhibit black American political, commercial, and rhetorical agency. Cary begins his argument by impugning black American agency in the context of white supremacy. Of an argument against emigration authored by prominent Philadelphian clergy, he writes: "I must say that the well selected and consistently arranged and proper adapted practical style which they used in bringing this address to a close— Prove to my satisfaction that they have learnt the use of words, but that they are obliged to use them in the wrong place, and at present gentlemen you are to the white people in America like our parrots are to us—using words without regard to the person or character to whom they are applied."[37] Cary's biting criticism suggests that although black Americans could imitate the style of American democracy, they would never master its spirit inside the United States, a political and cultural context saturated by racism.

In contrast, Cary characterized Africa as an inversion of all that can be known and done in North America. He described Canada, the Western territories, and Haiti—all alternatives for African emigration—as poor candidates because they already have governments and populations. He suggested that emigration to Africa is superior to these alternatives because it allowed for the creation of government where *no prior government existed.* Cary suggested that the space that would become Liberia, because it has no *Western* government, had no government at all. It was an empty and pure space whose resources waited for management. Throughout this articulation of space, commerce, and government, Cary maintained his faith in the principles of the American Revolution. Emigration to Liberia provided the opportunity to replicate the political and economic advances achieved by America's founders. Just as America was an empty space for the Puritans and English colonists, Africa was pure and waiting for African American emigration. What is remarkable about this

rhetoric is how it replicates the imperialist assumptions of mainstream
European discourse about Africa at the same time as it simultaneously
critiques the racism of the United States.

As Mary Louise Pratt documents in her study of nineteenth-century
travel literature about Africa, European authors traveled to Africa and
produced visions of the continent for the entertainment of European
imaginations. Pratt theorizes the multiplicity of "othering" strategies that
emerge from this discourse, the variety "of (seemingly) fixed positions and
the variety of (seemingly) given sets of differences." Ultimately, however,
this discourse articulated an essentialized Africa available for exploitation
by European capital. For example, Pratt's analysis of John Borrow's 1801
*Account of Travels into the Interior of Southern Africa in the years 1797 and
1798* demonstrates a tendency to reduce human action to a function of the
foreign environment. The drama of Borrow's work "is produced not by
the adventures of the travelers but by the changing 'face of the country.'
Signs of human presence, when they occur, are also expressed as marks
upon this face; the human agents responsible for those signs are themselves rarely seen." In contrast, Pratt identifies a sentimentalist tendency
in this discourse that valorizes the agency of the individual explorer. This
tradition relies upon heroic, epic narratives and is associated with "that
critical sector of the bourgeois world, the private sphere, home of the soli-
tary, introspecting individual."[38]

Lott Cary's interpretation of Africa resonates with both of these tendencies. First, in Cary's argument for African colonization, Africa is a
resource. Human behavior within this context is overdetermined by
Africa's boundless commercial potential. Thus, indigenous Africans are
seen as commercial resources and African American potential is as un-
limited as Africa's bounty. Second, however, African American colonization is heroic. Emigration itself is characterized as a quest for economic
advancement, human dignity, and moral advancement. The emigrationist
is a "race" hero. Moreover, Cary's characterization of Africa replicates the
center–periphery dynamic fundamental to the discourse of colonialism.
Although Cary's vision of African colonization does not emphasize the
importation of Christianity to civilize African populations, it does suggest that African Americans will bring entrepreneurial and organizational
skills to Africa. Cary's plan for emigration suggests that black Americans
will be managers and governors of African spaces and populations and
thus import the prospects of modernity from metropole to periphery.

The symmetry between Cary's rhetoric and that of colonialism's administrators can be explained by the work of sociologist Bernard Magubane. In *The Ties That Bind: African American Consciousness of Africa,* Magubane argues that colonialist characterizations of Africans and African space devalue black American experience and that white supremacist reductions of Africa are fundamental to European and African American expressions of community. Magubane's argument denies any tidy distinction between European and black American expressive traditions where they pertain to black America and the African Diaspora. Black Americans have intervened and reconfigured "Africa," but, fundamentally, Magubane argues, "New World" African American rhetoric imagines Africa through the semiotic frame of Western discourse.[39] Differences exist, but they do not reverse many of the fundamental ideological assumptions that Europeans used to construct a perspective on Africa's identity.

While Cary's rhetoric repeats some of the discursive strategies used by Europeans and European Americans, it also interjects difference by inverting some of the foundational narratives of colonialism. First, Cary uses the language of colonialism to criticize black American experience within the United States. His indictment of black American agency implies that African Americans suffer a colonial condition. In Cary's critical vision, colonialist policies unfairly subjugate black America and, implicitly, treat Africans in America like a "primitive" people.

Second, colonial discourse usually described the process of colonialism and colonization as a kind of divine duty to civilize savage spaces or as an economic project to bring fame, glory and wealth to one's country. While each of these rhetorical strategies operated with a logic of pure whiteness, they imagined colonial projects as other directed, i.e. colonialism should be practiced for the good of the oppressed or the health of a "nation." Despite Cary's own deeply held Christian beliefs, evangelism is noticeably absent in his argument for emigration. Rather, he argues for emigration in bald, selfish terms of economic advantage and escape from the racism of the United States.

Third, Cary himself is a subaltern whose identity has been constructed by a colonial white force; he is a product of colonialism, an object created by Western subjectivity. But his plans for colonization have no intention of bringing glory or wealth to his home country. He wants to exploit a new state not for the service of another, God or those who are to be converted/exploited, but for himself and his race. He does not pretend to anything other than empire building. In this case, however, he makes claim to an empire that includes people of color, an Africa composed of Africans and black Americans.

Buoyed by a progressive humanitarian impulse to deny the tenacity of white supremacy, Cary emigrated to Africa, his ideal space of commercial and symbolic power. Cary designed his colonial presence after the Southern plantation, including a slave class of indigenous Africans known as "recaptives." Only a few years after composing this letter, Cary was killed defending his compound from a recaptive rebellion. Despite his radical and progressive agenda, Cary's rhetorical colonialism, his arguments for economic, social, and spiritual development of the African Diaspora, were confounded by the horror and violence of the actual practices of colonialism.

The Politics of Black Anticolonialism

Just as Lott Cary argued for emigration to West Africa, European and African American abolitionists were becoming increasingly skeptical about the intentions and practices of the corporation that sponsored Cary's relocation—the American Colonization Society. As the free black population increased, European Americans began to view colonization as a possible solution to their own political and economic problems. Euro-American politicians who agreed on little else saw in colonization the opportunity for economic growth and fulfillment of the republican ideal, the removal of the divisive and potentially radical presence of free black bodies, and the creation of a homogeneous political space.[40] However, as European Americans lobbied for African American colonization, black American enthusiasm waned, and progressives directed their energies toward political improvement closer to home. Some prominent people of African descent argued that respectability and freedom could be achieved domestically though organizations that facilitated social improvement like the African Methodist Episcopal Church, while others advocated the establishment of independent black communities on this side of the Atlantic, in the territories, Canada, or on the island of Haiti. In the late 1820s emigration was largely unpopular in black communities, being considered impractical in the South and a distraction from righteous abolitionist activities in the North.[41] Thus, Cary occupied a problematic rhetorical space not only because of his complicity with the rhetoric of colonialism but also because he suffered as an advocate for a practice that many believed only benefited white supremacy.

Still, for Cary and other emigrationists in the first half of the nineteenth century, emigration was an element of a progressive rhetoric. The paucity of domestic political and economic opportunities and the seeming abundance of the same in Africa were incentives to emigration. Colonization also refuted the fallacies on which U.S. racial politics rested and manifested black political agency. In the early nineteenth century, each successful African colonist, male or female, embodied a moral potential foreclosed by repressive racial ideologies and inspired others to uplift the race, to fulfill the promises, requirements, and responsibilities of a modern community.

Emigration also offered the advantage of a particular location for black nationality. Most emigrationist rhetoric focused black identity in the spaces and states of the African Diaspora. Characterizations of black American difference, so long denigrated by U.S. rhetorics of white supremacy, were revalued through an association with African Diasporic spaces, which often vanished as emigrationists assumed the alabaster ethos of frontiersman.

Lott Cary was one of several prominent black Americans in the first half of the nineteenth century who looked to the globe for respite from domestic inequity and in so doing articulated a complex understanding of black nationality. Early black emigrationists explored where a black nation should be located, how it should sustain itself, and what should be its relationship to the European America in which it was imagined. These themes continued in the latter half of the nineteenth century, especially in the rhetoric of Martin Delaney, Henry Highland Garnet, Henry McNeal Turner, and others who frequently suggested that black political and economic growth could never occur within the borders of the United States. Perhaps the most influential of these voices were those of Edward Wilmont Blyden and Alexander Crummel.

Blyden argued that the people of the African Diaspora should "return" to Africa, but émigrés ought to be dark-skinned. In his vision, skin color signified a racial purity that he interpreted as an indicator of potential African identity. Put differently, Blyden viewed the hue of one's skin as a barometer of the degree to which a person could develop African identity. The health of the African race depended upon close proximity to African space and intimacy with its cultural traditions; the African Diaspora needed to return to a geographic and genetic African origin. Blyden understood emigration as mutually beneficial to African and black American populations, but articulated discrete benefits and responsibilities for each population.

Blyden's contemporary Alexander Crummel also articulated an essential space for Africa in black ethos. To Crummel, African cultural particularity signified difference from the West's anti-Christian decadence. Crummel believed that in separating black Americans from their African origins and exposing a segment of the African Diaspora to Christianity, slavery had created the possibility of the entire race's redemption from paganism and disempowerment — a perspective Wilson Jeremiah Moses describes as the doctrine of the "fortunate fall," the belief that slavery was redemptive. Moses suggests that the fortunate fall narrative helped emigrationists to navigate tensions between U.S. oppression and their hope for the racial community. In addition, fortunate fall arguments negotiated proximity with the United States and its foreign policy. The rhetoric of the fortunate fall rationalized black America's New World heritage into an imperative for African American leadership of the African continent. Crummel, like Blyden and other postbellum emigrationists, included Africa and the entire diaspora in the ethos of black America.[42]

Blyden and Crummel were not in perfect agreement about all issues faced by the African Diaspora, but their rhetoric about the relationship between people of African descent and the African continent, like Lott Cary's before it, included Africa within the boundaries of black identity, yet was ambivalent about the continent's indigenous population and political structures. In much of this rhetoric, Africa was described in the negative, characterized as a space free from restrictions on the development of black American economic power or as an absence of racial ambiguity. This definitional framework allowed New World Africans to view Africa in relation to their own experiences with racism. In the early years of the twentieth century this rhetorical characterization of Africa became increasingly important in black public argument in the New World.

CHAPTER 2

Black Ethos and the Rhetoric of Pan-Africa

IN THE PREVIOUS CHAPTER, I sketched a history of imperialism and identified the politics and cultural practices with which colonialism operates. I argued that colonialist practices were founded on the belief that cultures were distinct and that commerce between them occurred through diffusion. According to the diffusionist paradigm, a more developed "metropolitan" culture always existed at the spatial "center" of world-historical narratives. Cultures on the periphery evolved to higher stages of civilization through imitation of the metropole. In return, the periphery supplied the metropole with raw goods like labor or natural resources. In economic terms, this relationship was asymmetrical, because the manufactured goods that were exported from the metropole, like rum, had more value than the raw materials that were imported, such as sugar. Culturally, the export of Christianity and Western civilization to a pagan and "uncivilized" periphery figured in a similar equation. Because of the asymmetry inherent in this relationship, metropolitan cultures often viewed its commerce with the periphery in terms of national sacrifice. This sense of a sacrifice was heightened by the common belief that the periphery carried with it the danger of contamination; thus, colonial policies manipulated intercourse between discrete cultural spaces in an effort to keep them separate.

In this chapter, I introduce a second context, a discursive scene that outlines the role of diffusionist assumptions in the expression of black nationality in the early years of the twentieth century. The scope and purpose of this chapter make impossible a comprehensive history of Black

Nationalism or of how and when characterization of Africa has appeared in black public address generally.[1] Regardless, such a survey would not give adequate critical purchase on the particular rhetoric that shaped black identity at the outset of the twentieth century. Equally important, many prominent themes in this rhetorical history, especially the tropes and arguments that were most significant in the nineteenth century, reached their maturity at the beginning of the twentieth century, resounding most loudly and persuasively in the voices of black leaders.

The point of this chapter is not to indict black rhetoric for fanciful or regressive interpretations of Africa as has Tunde Adeleke.[2] Adeleke's argument, that nineteenth-century African American activists not only employed colonialist assumptions when they imagined Africa but also that they were complicit in colonialist policies, is deeply problematic in a number of ways, not the least of which is that it ignores the fundamentally dialogic nature of pan-Africanism. In contrast, Wilson Jeremiah Moses's groundbreaking *Afrotopia: The Roots of African American Popular History* appreciates the complexity of pan-Africanism and its negotiation of diverse, sometimes conflicting, ideological positions and cultural traditions. However, Moses's intellectual history does not focus on the connection between this cultural work and its political contexts and rhetorical effects.

Throughout the nineteenth century, elements of African culture persevered in black America through personal memories and cultural practices that endured slavery and racist policies.[3] This heritage and the twin colonial projects to de-Africanize African America and to manipulate African culture encouraged black Americans to invoke and revalue Africa in early expressions of black identity.[4] However, as the principle of diffusion structured the modern nation, it also shaped how many New World Africans expressed the character of black public community.[5] Black rhetoric during this period confronted, configured, and conformed to the principle of diffusion as it interpreted Africa and its diaspora.

In the early years of the twentieth century Africa's role in black identity underwent fundamental change in its tenor and scope. W. E. B. Du Bois and Marcus Garvey were at the forefront of this transformation, and their debate about Africa and its diaspora uniquely influenced black culture and politics. This chapter analyzes the rhetoric of Du Bois and Garvey's arguments about the nature of Africa and how it should matter for black people in diaspora. I argue that, through their public pronouncements about Africa, Du Bois and Garvey tried to craft a new "sense of place" for black people in which Africa was central; in so doing, they encouraged their audiences to understand black identity as performed in an international arena. This new perspective shifted the circumference of black experience away from the political borders created by white supremacy — indeed, away from the traditional boundaries that demarcate a state. Yet, despite this progressive frame, their rhetoric also reproduced the diffusionist assumptions of contemporaneous nationalist and colonialist projects; by this I mean that Du Bois and Garvey assumed a linear, asymmetrical mode of commerce between pure, core, and peripheral cultural spaces intranationally (between black social classes) and internationally (between New and Old World Africans). Ultimately, I argue that the rhetoric of Du Bois and Garvey constitutes Africa as an existential resource, and that black ethos, the context in which black character was formed, becomes metaphysical, a ground of coordinate essences rather than shared political conditions.

The Ethos of Black Identity

A number of scholars in rhetorical studies have theorized about how a "sense of place" informs rhetorical practice. The essays in *The Ethos of Rhetoric,* edited by Michael Hyde, ground this project in critical and theoretical exploration of the pre-Aristotelian meaning of the term "ethos." *Ethea,* from which "ethos" is derived, referred to a cave in which one dwelt. It then took on the meaning of the habits one formed within that cave. Eventually, through Aristotle, "ethos" came to signify instrumental virtue in a public sphere. Hyde's invigoration of ethos liberates the term from its strictly individualistic and instrumental senses. Ethos, in Hyde's register, refers to collective concerns and cultural contexts in which subjectivity is formed rather than in the strategic ambitions of an individual.

Hyde returns to the earliest sense of ethos and explores its significance for contemporary scholarship in rhetorical studies. He suggests that the "ethos of rhetoric" refers to "the way discourse is used to transform space and time into 'dwelling places' (ethos; pl. ethea) where people can deliberate about and 'know together' (con-scientia) some matter of interest. Such dwelling places define the grounds, the abodes or habitats, where a person's ethics and moral character take form and develop."[6] Ethos, in this sense, encompasses the cultural practices that create and perpetuate the topoi of cultural invention. Moreover, it refers to the fundamentally situated nature of those topoi: all rhetorical practices emerge from a point in time and a sense of place that are themselves constituted in discourse. The "ethos of rhetoric," then, highlights how locality is a foundation for public expression and political culture.

Hyde's articulation of ethos is useful to rhetorical critics for a number of reasons. It elevates the status of aesthetics and culture in rhetorical criticism and admonishes critics to attend to how language creates the conditions of public deliberation. It also focuses critical attention on the role of rhetorical time and space in the constitution of collective and individual identities; "ethos" names the processes and practices through which rhetoric configures the environments in which people come to know themselves and discuss public concerns. Last, the term "ethos" provides a vocabulary for treatment of the rhetorical effect of collective identity formation.

This sense of a "dwelling place" is particularly well suited for exploring rhetoric about racial politics because the tenacity and ubiquity of white supremacy have created a fundamentally inhospitable "dwelling place" for communities "marked" by race.[7] Moreover, rhetorical practices that seek to influence racial politics often police the boundaries of cultural spaces or propose alternative spaces in which progressive communities can be imagined. Eric King Watts, in his essay "The Ethos of a Black Aesthetic: An Exploration of Larry Neal's Visions of a Liberated Future," analyzes the expression of an African American dwelling place in the rhetoric of the Black Arts Movement. Watts treats Larry Neal's "Visions of a Liberated Future" as emblematic of the Black Arts Movement's independent black aesthetic. The Black Arts aesthetic imagined a distinctly black way of being in the world that confronted white supremacy and provided a new framework for self-awareness.[8] As a "frame-work," the Black Arts aesthetic illustrated how individuals use rhetoric to shape the discursive context in which a community imagines its being in the world; from this perspective, The Black Arts Movement is important not only because of its aesthetic innovations but also because it created a new context for understanding black experience and realizing black community. Individuals of African descent have also invoked the African Diaspora in rhetoric that performs this function. This expression of an African or Afro-Diasporic "dwelling place" is often studied through the vocabulary of "Pan-Africanism."

Pan-Africanism

According to Immanuel Geiss, Pan-Africanism is "among the most complex but also vague phenomena in modern history."[9] Not surprisingly, scholars have defined Pan-African activity in a number of ways.[10] Moreover, texts and movements that could be considered "Pan-African" have been studied though alternative vocabularies—Black Nationalism, African Nationalism, the African Personality, St. Clair Drake's "Africa Interest," or the contemporary turn to the theoretical term "diaspora," to name a few.[11] Given the many definitions of and approaches to Pan-Africanism, I posit that the term is best understood analytically, as an umbrella term that encompasses diverse expressions of solidarity between Africans and the African Diaspora and the effort to create an international "home" for populations of African descent.

The academic study of Pan-Africanism flourished in the 1960s as scholars attempted to provide a historical context for the growth of Africa's political independence. In 1962 George Shepperson traced a genealogy of Pan-African thought in order to distinguish two varieties: Pan-Africanism and pan-Africanism.[12] Shepperson described Pan-Africanism as the specific political movement initiated by Henry Sylvester Williams in 1900 at the First Pan-Africa Conference and continued under the leadership of W. E. B. Du Bois in subsequent conventions. In contrast, pan-Africanism was "not a clearly recognizable movement, with a single nucleus." Rather, it was a "group of movements, many very ephemeral," in which the "cultural element often predominates."[13] Other scholars, such as Immanuel Geiss and Wilson Jeremiah Moses, have drawn a similar distinction between political and cultural "Pan-Africanisms."[14] Indeed, for many years the relationship between politics and culture was the central problematic of Pan-Africanist activism and scholarship.

Contemporary scholars reject this dichotomy between cultural and political Pan-Africanisms. Afrocentric scholars emphasize an Afro-Diasporic political imperative within cultural Pan-Africanism. Michael W. Williams, for example, defines Pan-Africanism by dissociating it from Zionism. Williams asserts that Pan-Africanism is ethnically and racially contiguous whereas Zionism admits heterogeneity; that Pan-Africanism is inherently anti-imperial while Zionism is a neocolonial endeavor; and that Pan-Africanism is socialist while Zionism only feigns desire for a classless society as part of its acquisitive agenda.[15] In a similar vein, Kwame

Nantambu argues that the term "panafricanism" is itself ideologically suspect. He contends that panafricanism is a Eurocentric concept that divorces Pan-African sentiment from its radical and revolutionary program.[16] Interestingly, both of these formulations of Pan-Africanism are remarkably ahistorical, because they rely upon a philosophically and ontologically pure sense of Africanity that preexists history.

In the introduction to their anthology *Imagining Home: Class, Culture, and, Nationalism in the African Diaspora,* Sidney J. Lemelle and Robin D. G. Kelly also deny the distinction between the cultural and political work of Pan-African thought, but they argue for a deeply historical approach to Pan-African activity.[17] Accordingly, the essays collected in this volume treat Pan-Africanism as an assortment of movements both cultural and political. These movements are distinctly "Pan-African" because they confront the oppression of Africans (in Africa and in the African Diaspora) and represent a stage in the historical evolution of the black struggle for freedom. This definition of "Pan-Africanism" pivots on a particularly modern understanding of progress and social change. In the final essay of the anthology, "The Politics of Cultural Existence: Pan-Africanism, Historical Materialism, and Afrocentricity," Lemelle contends that progress is the result of history itself, not of "ideas" like cultural identity.[18] In Lemelle's Marxist register, cultural identity is an aftereffect of history; pan-African identity is a consequence of the transnational black struggle against colonialism rather than a motivating force within that struggle.

Afrocentric and Marxist approaches to Pan-Africanism perpetuate the very distinction between culture and politics that they explicitly set out to rebut — the Afrocentric approach viewing Pan-Africanism as the political work of a culture that preceded history and the Marxist approach treating culture as the residue of politics. Rhetorical analysis provides a middle ground between these two trends in the study of Pan-African activity. A rhetorical perspective does not assume the a priori existence of cultural community, nor does it deny the significance of cultural identity in motivating political change.

Scholars in rhetorical studies have yet to explore the history of Pan-African rhetorical practice. The only recent rhetorical scholarship that explores Pan-African rhetoric, a book chapter by Robert Terrill and Eric King Watts titled "W. E. B. Du Bois, Double Consciousness, and Pan-Africanism in the Progressive Era," traces the development of Du Bois's understanding of "double consciousness" during the first twenty-five years of the twentieth century. Terrill and Watts argue that double conscious-ness is a primary trope of Du Boisian thought. In his earliest work, Du Bois used double consciousness to describe the productive tensions that arise in between polarities like mass and elite, public and private, and black and white. Terrill and Watts contend that Du Bois reconfigured "double consciousness" in the late teens and early 1920s. As he attempted to distinguish his internationalism from that of Marcus Garvey, Du Bois understood double consciousness in an international context. In this sense, double consciousness did not disappear from Du Bois's rhetoric; it evolved into a Pan-African vision defined by enduring tensions between "Africa" and "America."[19]

Although fine scholarship, this piece is primarily an intellectual his-tory of Du Bois's developing thought and not an explication of Pan-African rhetorical practice per se. Terrill and Watts provide an invaluable illustration of the intellectual and rhetorical crucible in which Du Bois and Garvey debated the parameters of black identity in the early years of the twentieth century. Most notably, they demonstrate how Du Bois and Garvey articulated influential visions of black identity in which Africa played a central role. However, they do not explore the nature of that "African" presence and how that particular characterization of "Africa" influenced this new black ethos. My purpose is not to offer a definitive interpretation of Du Bois's or Garvey's Pan-African rhetoric, but instead to illustrate how rhetorical criticism of Pan-Africanist discourse can tease out the "ethos" or "dwelling place" of early twentieth-century black iden-tity. In short I analyze this rhetoric to ascertain the kind of "home" Pan-Africa represented and the implications this variety of home had for black politics during this era.

W. E. B. Du Bois and the Pan-African Ideal

At the turn of the century many racial progressives argued that black people could achieve domestic political change through the refinement of culture and the uplift of the black working class.[20] This uplift imperative required the dissemination of high culture from the middle-class core to the "uncivilized" periphery. The rhetoric of cultural and economic uplift that dominated black life at the turn of the century assumed a mass im-perative for the imitation of elite values.[21] Black mass culture was chang-ing rapidly. From 1910 to 1930 black American literacy leapt from 35 to 85 percent, the last generation born in slavery passed away, and middle-class communities in Harlem and Washington, D.C., flourished alongside recently displaced émigrés from the American South, the West Indies, and Africa.[22] Furthermore, inspired by the language of democracy employed to justify World War I, Japan's 1905 victory over the Russian Empire, nascent Irish nationalism, and the Russian Revolution, many black Americans came to see racism, imperialism, and strategies of resistance in an international context.[23] These developments in the first decades of the twentieth century enabled the expression of a new international black ethos focused on the idea of "culture."

W. E. B. Du Bois's Pan-African rhetoric developed at the intersection of these changes. Like his mentor Alexander Crummel, Du Bois believed that high culture could uplift the masses and improve the political condition of the race.[24] Du Bois also argued that U.S. racism and black American identity had international dimensions. However, by the second decade of the twentieth century, he focused his vision for racial uplift and the international struggle for human rights on Africa.[25] In 1915 Du Bois published an essay entitled "The African Roots of the War." This essay argued that the coming world war was motivated by Europe's greed for colonial acquisition in Africa. Five years later, in *Darkwater: Voices behind the Veil,* Du Bois revisited this theme and his earlier essay. The new version, a chapter entitled "The Hands of Ethiopia," clearly expressed Du Bois's vision of Africa, what it should become, and how that future should matter for Africans in diaspora.

In the beginning of his essay Du Bois challenges the belief that African history is peripheral to world history. In contrast to the assumption that "Africa is far afield from the center of our burning social problems," he argues that "always Africa is giving us something new or some metempsychosis of some world-old thing."[26] Later in the essay he contends that "Africa" is a paradigm of the human spirit because it has maintained this central space in world history despite a history of tribulation: "Out of them in days without date flowed the beginnings of Egypt. . . . They have fought every human calamity in its most hideous form and yet today hold some similar vestiges of a mighty past."[27] Du Bois characterizes Africa as neither an object nor an afterthought in world history, but as an actor that is central to its fundamental narratives. Indeed, in a 1914 essay he argued that *all* civilization itself grew from an African origin: "Africa is distinctly the land of the mother. . . . This does not seem to be solely the survival of the historic matriarchy through which all nations pass. It appears to be more than this, as if the black race in passing down steps of human culture gave the world not only the Iron Age, the cultivation of the soil and the domestication of animals but also in peculiar emphasis the mother-idea."[28] Du Bois's argument for an African origin of civilization was complex; he posited a pure, uncomplicated space from which cultural complexity could emanate to an imitating periphery, and in so doing replicated the form of the diffusionist assumptions that structured much racially regressive anthropology of the era.

In the heyday of colonial expansion, cultural evolution often was explained in terms of internal or external development. For example, cultures were thought to change because of autonomous innovation or the influence of externalities like exposure to other cultures through war, missionary efforts, or cross-cultural commerce. These theories of culture, called "independent invention" and "diffusionism" respectively, grew from divergent assumptions about the nature of human society. Independent invention privileged the autonomy of a culture and the relative impermeability of its borders. Diffusionism, on the other hand, assumed that human societies were essentially imitative and that cultural transmission was unidirectional. According to the diffusionist paradigm, under colonialism the Western core developed the static or empty colonial periphery; the West possessed historical agency while Asia, Africa, and the indigenous Americas imitated its example, developing economically, politically, and spiritually through association with Western cultures. In the United States, the popularity of diffusionist theorizing peaked during turn-of-the-century debates about U.S. imperialism and isolationism. Diffusionism as an explanation for cultural difference declined in mass popularity from the 1920s to the post–World War II period. After World War I, "progress" enjoyed less persuasive authority. However, many scholars continued to debate the relative merits of diffusionism, and the model continued to exert a powerful influence on foreign policy discourse and political judgment. In the 1930s several European American anthropologists adopted a form of "extreme" diffusionism in which they argued that all culture emanated from one originating point. G. Eliot Smith, for example, in his 1933 book, *The Diffusion of Culture,* argued that all culture could trace its roots to ancient Egypt and Phoenicia. Smith's identification of a geographic source from which civilization spread throughout human history paralleled the spatial relationships upon which colonialism relied; the valorization of colonized spaces as "the origin" was not incompatible with their exploitation of those spaces.[29]

Clearly, Du Bois's argument about Africa replicated some of these contemporaneous assumptions. Du Bois understood Africa in evolutionary terms, as a primitive antecedent to European modernism. As Eric King Watts demonstrates, Du Bois's depiction of the "primitive" progressively equated an African origin with Europe's classical foundations.[30] Du Bois also refuted contemporaneous evaluations of Africa that dissociated populations of the African Diaspora from African history; confronting Josiah Nott, George Gliddon, and Egyptologist James Breasted, Du Bois argued that ancient Africa had been populated by a black race. Furthermore, he implied that the descendents of ancient Africa were now enduring racial prejudice in Africa and the United States.[31] In this way, Du Bois confronted and reconfigured diffusionist assumptions even as he employed them.

For Du Bois, then, ancient Africa provided the foundation of both Western civilization and African culture. Because they inherited technologies and the "mother-idea" from ancient Africa, Western civilization and contemporary Africans existed in debt to a historical entity. At this stage in Du Bois's intellectual career, ancient Africa was the source of an excellence that could not be replicated in his day—it could only be respected in the past or aspired to in the future.

As "The Hands of Ethiopia" continues, Du Bois argues that the end of World War I presented two possible futures for the world, each defined by what Africa would become. In one future, Africa would continue to be exploited through colonial policies for the economic benefit of Europe. In contrast, citing incipient movements toward self-determination in Ireland and Poland, he suggested a preferable future in which Europe would help Africa to consolidate and form a single black community.

Du Bois's argument for an Africa for Africans targeted European policy makers and those who might influence European and U.S. policy toward Africa, but it implied benefits for both Europe and the African Diaspora. He cast his proposed African state as a challenge to the spirit of Europe, an opportunity for colonial powers to prove their good intentions—indeed, their civilization. Du Bois argued, "world philanthropy, like national philanthropy, must come as uplift and prevention, not merely as alleviation and religious conversion. Reverence for humanity, as such, must be installed in the world, and Africa should be the talisman."[32] At this point in the text, Du Bois extrapolated the ideology of uplift from the domestic scene to an international one. He translated an imperative for the uplift of the black masses into a warrant for the development of Africa.

This uplift of Africa would occur through a colonial agency. Despite Du Bois's critique of European imperialism, he is explicitly ambivalent about colonialism in this text. For instance, he praises colonialism for its progressive impact on Africa, pointing out that "missionaries and commerce have left some good with their evil," namely, the proliferation of mission schools. Moreover, he proposes that the future African state should be designed according to the "example of the best colonial administrators."[33] He also suggests that colonial practices are evil because of their mobilization toward economic exploitation, not in and of themselves, nor for what they imply about the African communities upon whom they are enacted.

Du Bois does not explicitly describe what this new black state would mean for blacks in the African Diaspora. Still, he makes it clear that the new black state would have some special significance for Africans in diaspora that is cultural rather than political in nature. He contends that black people in the African Diaspora have "earned the right to fight out their problems where they are, but they could easily furnish from time to time technical experts, leaders of thought, and missionaries of culture for their backward brethren in the new Africa."[34] Black people in the African Diaspora should not look to this new African state as a space in which to enact political authority; nor is it necessarily going to evolve into a font of future political power for the race as a whole. In this way, Du Bois delineates cultural identity between Africans and the African Diaspora while at the same time underscoring political difference.

The text demonstrates that Du Bois's understanding of black ethos continued to distinguish between inhabitants of Africa and the United States in significant ways. This distinction centered on the basis of differing political agendas. And yet these differing agendas were not equal, for he privileged the Western core. Africa needed to achieve autonomy, but black America needed to labor on behalf of itself and Africa as well. New World blacks were in debt to an ideal.

Du Bois suggests that the political battle for black rights is a domestic one. However, black *culture* passes through these borders; black people may be engaged in distinct political projects but they share a past and future. As Africa provides a chance for the redemption of colonialism as a test of European civilization, it provides a similar test for black people in the African Diaspora. In a 1919 issue of *The Advocate of Peace,* he argued that "the African Movement (Pan-Africanism) must mean to us what the Zionist movement must mean to the Jews, the centralization of a race effort and the recognition of a racial front."[35]

Du Bois's vision of Africa affects black ethos in the following ways. First, it is a fundamentally international appreciation of the terrain of black identity. Even though Du Bois implies that black people in the diaspora live in distinct political contexts, they share a future and a community that transcends nation and state. In this sense, he articulates, not just a new black identity, but a new stage on which black identity can be performed; black politics are domestic, but black culture is an international phenomenon.[36] Second, within this international context, discrete black populations have distinct political responsibilities to ensure the health of the race. A singular, independent Africa is the goal that defines black community, but populations within this context have particular political charges. In this sense, Du Bois' stratified his vision of the space of Black Nationalism; at the top were a core of cultural elites who inspired and then led the mass of Africa toward high cultural ideals. In 1897 he argued that African Americans, the "advance guard of the Negro people," should remember their association with the African Diaspora and "take their just place in the vanguard of pan-negroism."[37]

Du Bois attempted to create an organization that would speed the formation of this advance guard. Following Henry Sylvester Williams's Pan-African Conference in 1900, Du Bois organized Pan-African conferences in 1917, 1922, and 1934. Elite diasporic and African blacks attended these conferences, where they formed relationships and discussed the fortunes of the race in an international context. However, these meetings stopped short of recommending self-determination for African states. Indeed, their political impact was negligible relative to their symbolic function. For Du Bois, "Africa" was a mythic origin and a symbolic goal; his Pan-Africanism was a recuperative project that sought to "elevate" black America and the African Diaspora to the prospects of these past and future conditions.[38]

Marcus Garvey's African Empire

Du Bois's rival Marcus Garvey expressed a related yet distinct vision of Pan-African ethos. Garvey, too, rhetorically intervened in the discourse of white supremacy with a new, international frame for black collective identity. Indeed, Garvey and Du Bois were often conflated in popular discourse, both considered icons of a single Pan-African movement.[39] However, while Du Bois's vision of Africa grew from the discourse of cultural uplift, Garvey's rhetoric of Pan-African community developed within the context of an emerging black proletarian class.[40] Although his Pan-African ethos reflected this commitment to labor, it, too, structured the space of black nationality through diffusionist assumptions.

In the United States the great migration north created urban poverty and distressed organizations that provided social services.[41] New organizations formed to minister to the economic and political needs of this displaced population, foremost among which was Marcus Garvey's Universal Negro Improvement Association. Garvey conjoined Booker T. Washington's philosophy of self-help to a theory of African community. His vision united the self-interest of the black American individual, the self-interest of black America, and the self-interest of the entire African Diaspora in a plea for global racial chauvinism.[42] His desire to arouse racial chauvinism was influenced by sociologist Robert Park (through Booker T. Washington, whom Park served as secretary).

To Park, every human community was like an organism. Nature existed not in a static balance, but as a process of continuous change punctuated by moments of disruption. In this sense, human populations grew in a manner similar to those of plants and animals: through competition. Particular cultural identities were essential to allow cultures to compete with each other. Cultural identity grew from struggles between groups over resources; and cultural nationalism was a strategic good that facilitated that competition. Park applied sociological theories of immigrant assimilation to black communities recently migrated to the urban north. He argued that the creation of race had hindered the competitive potential of black and Asian American populations. The stigma of difference affected individual pride and self-concept, making certain populations less able to compete with communities not so marked. Most important, the root of the deleterious effects of racial difference was in the tendency to erase the individual. Individuals from groups marked with race were doomed to serve as synecdoches for their race and never be treated as individuals. Park lauded the chauvinistic economic practices of recently arrived European immigrants and praised the creation of black dolls in 1924. Nationalism and the deliberate creation of cultural identity were justifiable, even essential, tactics in the competition between groups, because differences between racial groups and similarities within the same could be used to mobilize political and moral efficacy in response to social crisis.

Like many who endure the colonial condition, Garvey first came to "race" consciousness while in the "mother" country. As a young man living in London, Garvey read *Ethiopia Unbound: Studies in Race Emancipation* by J. E. Casely Hayford and Duse Muhammad Ali's diffusionist history *In the Land of the Pharaohs,* and came to expect the coming of a "new world of black men, not peons, serfs, dogs and slaves, but a nation of sturdy men making their impress upon civilization and causing a new light to dawn upon the human race."[43] A rejuvenated, redeemed Africa played a central role in Garvey's prophecy.

In a 1923 essay entitled "African Fundamentalism," Garvey describes Africa and what it should mean for the masses of the African Diaspora. At the beginning of the essay, he argues for a new African symbology, contending that black people must "inspire a literature and promulgate a doctrine of our own without any apologies to the powers that be."[44] Garvey's rhetorical characterization of Africa in this essay is part of this symbolic project to create a foundation for transnational African community.

Here Garvey employs "Africa" as a frame for understanding Western civilization. Much like Du Bois, he avers that African civilization preceded European civilization. Also like Du Bois, Garvey interprets this temporal preeminence as proof that Western civilization derived from an African source. He declares that when ancient Africa was embracing the arts and sciences on the banks of the Nile, Euro-America's ancestors "were still drinking human blood and eating out of the skulls of their conquered dead; when our civilization had reached the noonday of progress, they were still running naked and sleeping in holes and caves with rats, bats, and other animals."[45] Later he contends that "their [Europe's] modern improvements are but duplicates of a grander civilization that we had thousands of years ago, without the advantage of what is buried and still hidden to be resurrected and reintroduced by the intelligence of our generation and our posterity."[46]

These claims critique Western imperialism by exposing its absence of independent invention, but they also demonstrate Garvey's theory of how cultures relate to each other. In this and other texts he contends that cultures develop through imitation of other cultures. In a speech he gave November 11, 1923, Garvey advocated imitation of the "white" model of

imperialism, implying that it would be desirable for this model to be diffused, first to New World black Christians and then, through their agency,
to the rest of the African Diaspora. Claiming that the white man is the
"standard of man" and an exemplar to be emulated, he suggests: "whatsoever [white] man has done we must do." To provide evidence of this standard, Garvey articulates a hierarchy of culture. He states that "The white
man has changed the wilderness into the beautiful nations of England
and France and Germany and Italy and Spain and Russia and Austria and
Hungary" and subsequently lists the "beautiful and wonderful" nations
of North, Central, and South America. The paragraph is structured so
as to give temporal and qualitative superiority to European nations. The
modern skill to consume nature began with the Europeans, was learned
subsequently by North Americans, then spread to South America. Black
America's proximity to the source of this historical agency, Europe, creates
distance from contemporary Africans and distinct responsibilities within
the context of an African diaspora.[47]

Despite Garvey's anticolonial agenda and outreach to diverse African
communities, his vision of Africa was fundamentally reductive, employed
imperialist imagery, and expressed an ambivalent relationship with colonialism. In a 1921 essay entitled "Africa for the Africans" Garvey rebuked
U.S. race leaders who suggested that black Americans were not suited to
the African climate. He argued that New World blacks were removed
from Africa only by accident and that black Americans and Africans
shared a relationship to ancient civilization in African history. There was
nothing, then, to inhibit African American and West Indian efforts to
build "a racial empire" in their own "motherland."[48] Indeed, Garvey had
argued that the people of the West Indies "will be the instruments of unit-
ing a scattered race who, before the close of many centuries will found
an empire on which the sun shall shine as ceaselessly as it shines on the
Empire of the North today."[49]

However, Garvey still characterized the founding of this empire as
an exercise in cooperation and admonished American and West Indian
blacks not to travel to Africa expecting "overlordship," but rather to import a duty to "establish in Africa that brotherly cooperation which will
make the interests of the native African and the American and West Indian Negro one and the same."[50] Nonetheless, as is evident through his
use of terms like "motherland" and "empire," Garvey's vision of Africa was
indebted to the rhetoric of Western imperialism. He suggested that the

work of empire building included the Christianization and the "civilization of the backward tribes of Africa."[51] Indeed, he claimed that he worked
and prayed for "the establishing of a great and binding racial empire . . .
whose only natural, spiritual, and political limits shall be God and Africa,
at home and abroad."[52]

Garvey's vision of Africa translates into a sense of black ethos that is
founded upon a single racial destiny, but this destiny is bifurcated by the
responsibilities of particular peoples within the African Diaspora. Africa
is a resource for the diaspora, its history is the foundation, its future is the
destiny; but contemporary Africa is an impediment.

Both Du Bois and Garvey argued for new frameworks in which to understand black community. They both believed that the political borders
created by white supremacy and colonialism were inauthentic parameters
of black identity. Their rhetoric posited that black identity occurred in
an international context. However, this international context was not
the space between states. Indeed, Du Bois and Garvey's characterizations
of Africa suggested that black identity was performed in a metaphysical
space above politics.

Pan-Africa and the Character of Black Ethos

The rhetoric of W. E. B. Du Bois and Marcus Garvey struggled to balance
the domestic and international, mass and elite, vernacular and institutional
dimensions of the collective identity of the African Diaspora. Ultimately,
the discourse of diffusionism, the language of cultural purity, origin, and
periphery structured these progressive expressions of black community.
This colonial dynamic of part to whole is a key to understanding the rhetorical function of interpreting the African Diaspora during this period.
Within this rhetoric the relationship between Africa and its diaspora is
configured synecdochically. Burke argues that synecdoche performs the
rhetorical function of representation. Through synecdoche, part stands
for "whole, whole for part, container for the thing contained."[53] In the
Pan-African rhetoric of Du Bois and Garvey, Africa "stands in" for the
future prospects of all people of African descent; "Africa" is the telos that
binds, the destiny that substitutes for the differences in cultural heritage
and political condition that exist between black people around the globe.
In a similar fashion, the African Diaspora stands in for the agency that
will pursue this goal.

Consequently, this discourse resulted in a largely hierarchal understanding of how cultures developed and a coordinately hierarchal understanding of how populations within a culture related to each other and developed. The black diaspora's potential was related to its labor on *behalf* of Africa; indeed, the progressive nature of political action relies on its logic of leader and follower. This pattern created a limitation for dealing with the cultures of the diaspora on truly equal terms and perpetrated fissures in black American culture between Christian black American and African "pagan," between the Victorian black middle class and the vulgar mass, and between ancient Africa and its present. In this sense, Pan-African rhetoric in the early years of the twentieth century inherited much from nineteenth-century precedent. Like his mentor Alexander Crummel, Du Bois valued Africa's classic past and prophesied social change through imitation of an ideal. Similarly, Garvey echoed the racial chauvinism of his hero Edward Wilmont Blyden when he argued for a transnational racial destiny grounded in metaphysical blackness.[54] In Du Bois and Garvey, these nineteenth-century arguments achieved new depth and impact.

The Pan-African rhetoric that Du Bois and Garvey represent served an existential function in black America that foreclosed the realization of a mass, reciprocal Afro-Diasporic community. The distinction between these two rhetorical functions, existential and political, parallels the distinction between what political theorist Carl Schmitt identifies as "the political" and "politics." In his 1927 book *The Concept of the Political,* Schmitt postulates a condition that antedates the struggle for specific policies. He calls this condition "the political." For him, the political is a metaphysical space, the place where identity is found. Within this space, communities are coherent due to their faith in an essential oneness. In Schmitt's political theology, community results from faith in ontological continuity and difference; geographic distance between people is transcended through metaphysical presence, and difference is a question of substance, of essence. Chantal Mouffe enlists Schmitt's opinions in her critique of liberal rationalism and universalism. She argues that Schmitt's sense of the political foregrounds the aesthetic dimensions of political community, the emotional investment that motivates and mobilizes political community, the feeling of togetherness that makes a particular political community compelling. Mouffe also employs Schmitt's idea to demonstrate the irreducibility of difference; every expression of sameness, of common cause, also excludes, and in so doing defines an "other" upon which the original sameness depends. She argues that this modern conceptualization of citizenship influenced how modern democracy took shape but also presented certain obstacles to pluralism, making it difficult for "a diverse collection of communities" to create "unity without denying specificity."[55]

The language of the "political" complicates how we understand rhetorical ethos as a "dwelling place." Namely, the topoi of cultural invention may be comprised of largely (though not exclusively) existential or political components. For example, the Pan-African rhetoric of W. E. B. Du Bois and Marcus Garvey that I have described illustrates the disposition of community constituted in a mostly existential framework. For the most part, the African Diaspora coheres around a debt to a glorious past, a future destiny, and an evolving notion of culture and race. All of these grounds involve faith in shared reference to a metaphysical category rather than through perception of a shared political condition. Indeed, the rhetoric discussed in this essay necessitates distinct political conditions in the realms of Africans, African Americans, and the African Diaspora. Geographical distance and ontological difference were negated through faith in metaphysical oneness.[56]

Moreover, the rhetoric of Du Bois and Garvey in the first quarter of the twentieth century patterned the existential terrain on the form of colonial discourse. The constitution of self and other, friend and enemy, reflected the dynamic of the metropole and the periphery in the diffusionist paradigm at the foundation of colonialist thinking. Indeed, a sense of essential difference, between black American Christians and pagan Africans, between middle-class black Americans and the lumpen proletariat, and between "modern" and "primitive" Africans, constituted the authenticity of black ethos. The space of cultural purity could only be accomplished on a metaphysical terrain. This configuration of black national space privileged intimacy with its source; skin color, practical experience with Africa, and the best interests of the African Diaspora as a whole figured as signs of genetic and cultural proximity to this epicenter of black experience.

A further example of the power and ubiquity of this rhetoric during this period can be seen in the case of Grover Cleveland Redding. Redding was a Chicago-based activist who by 1920 had built a small but committed movement, the Star Order of Ethiopia, also known as the Abyssinians.

Like many other advocates of the "Back to Africa" philosophies so popular during the 1920s, Redding's affiliation with Ethiopia was essentially mystical. He and his followers invented "Ethiopian" rituals and wore flowing white robes while they rode horses down Chicago's streets. He advocated emigration to Ethiopia, but his plan was neither practical nor fully articulated. The policy of emigration wasn't really the point. Rather, for Redding, Ethiopia was metaphysical, a space of a true and truly redemptive reality, a space wherein more authentic relationships could form between black people and between a black person and herself. Redding was so committed to this alternative metaphysical space that he granted no authority whatsoever to earthly political powers. In June 1920 he burned two U.S. flags while rallying against "America." At this rally, a white sailor and a black police officer, both representatives of the "state," took umbrage and a riot broke out. Both were killed. Redding was convicted of murder and sentenced to be hanged. His last words, "I have something to say, but not at this time," were defiant and suggested that he viewed his existence in a context other than those of the courtroom, the state's execution chamber, or the claustrophobic United States.[57]

No doubt Du Bois would have blanched at being compared with Grover Cleveland Redding and likely have become apoplectic at the suggestion that he had anything in common with Marcus Garvey. However, in his rhetoric about Africa's role in the dwelling places of black life, he had much in common with these other voices so prominent in the early years of the twentieth century. Indeed, as Wilson Jeremiah Moses argues, "Du Bois was in unacknowledged harmony with the Afrocentrism of his archrival, Marcus Garvey and such working-class cults as the Black Jews of Harlem and the Black Muslims"[58]

Garvey and Du Bois were among many black activists who actively configured and repurposed the rhetoric that created the modern nation. Black activists were neither passive objects of this discourse nor its unwitting imitators, as Garvey in particular is often accused of being. In the early years of the twentieth century, black rhetoric cast black collective identity as occurring on a world stage, one in which populations of African descent enjoyed increased opportunity for sympathy and empathy among diverse groups of people. Du Bois's and Garvey's rhetorics were instrumental in creating this context.

In this chapter I have traced the role of the discourse of diffusionism in how black America understood Africa and itself. I have argued that a

diffusionist logic of core and periphery, inherited from contemporaneous colonial and nationalist discourse, structured the space of black nationality. Employing this rhetorical frame as they interpreted the African
Diaspora, Du Bois and Garvey did so existentially, or in aid of securing
and stabilizing a sense of self through reference to a common metaphysical substance (the "race," its destiny, or a debt to a sense of civilization,
for example). As the 1920s drew to a close, innovations in how culture
could signify created the opportunity for people of African descent to
imagine the African Diaspora and the space of black nationality in more
coordinate, political terms. Public political expression also motivated and
was motivated by this transition in the discourse of culture. Responding
to political crises in Haiti, Liberia, and Ethiopia, people of African descent in the New World, horrified by the racism that saturated Western
imperialism, spoke out in an anticolonial voice that reduced geographic
distance between people of the African Diaspora but maintained the
particularity of its cultures. In the case studies that follow I explore how
the African Diaspora figured in this rhetoric during this shift, how this
discourse impacted black political behavior, and how it interacted with
rhetorics of white supremacy and black identity.

CHAPTER 3

"Unhappy Haiti"

U.S. Imperialism, Racial Violence, and the Politics of Diaspora

IN THE FIRST QUARTER of the twentieth century, people of African descent in the New World argued about what Africa could mean to its people in diaspora. These arguments took the form of speeches, essays, poems, newspapers, music, and visual art. By and large, much of this discourse operated within the same assumptions about the nature of culture and parameters of black public space that structured the Pan-African rhetoric of W. E. B. Du Bois and Marcus Garvey: black ethos was frequently expressed in terms of a spiritual unity, founded in Africa and distributed among the African Diaspora. Although many people of African descent did locate a part of their sense of personal identity in Africa, this identity did not extend to coherent political positions or an appreciation of shared political contexts. At the close of the 1920s, however, social circumstances in the United States and developments in the meaning of "culture" among the black elite enabled a rhetoric that simultaneously redefined Africa and the scope and style of black American participation in U.S. democracy. This rhetoric employed a new resource as well: U.S. foreign policy. Foreign policy issues like the occupation of Haiti by U.S. troops were perceived as crises in many black communities, and these crises provided an opportunity for black people to articulate a new collective identity based on an explicitly political affiliation with the African Diaspora, to pursue alternative strategies for progressive politics, and to oppose white supremacy both at home and abroad.

Haiti has a long history in U.S. rhetorical culture and black America. During the nineteenth century, Haiti and prominent Haitians figured in descriptions of the political potential of black Americans. For example, the leaders who achieved Haiti's independence, Toussaint-Louverture and Jean-Jacques Dessalines, appeared in U.S. discourse as two paradigms of black agency. Louverture represented the potential for republican government in the African Diaspora, and Dessalines embodied the power of violent revolution to establish cultural integrity.[1] In this allegorical register, mythic Haitian individuals provided political and moral ideals whose celebration inspired black people around the globe.

The actual state of Haiti, however, was a source of ambivalence in black America; the country's political instability and its legacy of French colonialism complicated how black Americans identified with the Caribbean nation. During much of the nineteenth century, Haiti struggled to accomplish peaceful transitions of political power and to maintain its economic and political autonomy in the face of European and U.S. imperial ambitions. Nineteenth-century emigrationist James Theodore Holly, who became a resident of Haiti in 1862, blamed this instability on the crippling legacies of the related evils colonialism and slavery, but he also argued that Haiti's French language and culture, Catholicism, and pagan voodoo had retarded the country's development. Holly lobbied for increased U.S. black emigration to create a more "Anglo-African" Haiti, imagining black America as an agent in Haiti's approach to the modern: the "Black Anglo-Saxon" would speed the cultural transformations necessary for Haiti's empowerment. Holly's complicated perspective saw intertwined destinies for black America and Haiti; nevertheless, these destinies would be possible only through the agency of the civilizing influence of black America. For Holly and many black Americans in the nineteenth century, Haiti was *both* a source of "expectation, pride, missionary zeal" and "embarrassment, despair, and irritation."[2]

When the United States occupied Haiti in 1915, many black Americans reinterpreted their relationship to the country. Unlike U.S. imperialism in Mexico and the Philippines, the invasion of Haiti generated moments of widespread, passionate response.[3] Many black Americans initially supported the occupation, because they believed that a military presence in Haiti was the first and necessary step in the country's transformative evolution toward a modern democracy. "Race" was largely an absent or ancillary dimension of these arguments about Haiti; the intervention itself was described as a matter of foreign policy rather than a policy that affected black America directly. As the occupation became increasingly violent and exploitative, however, black Americans saw it as being motivated by the same racism that perpetuated social inequality at home. The turning point for black American attitudes toward the occupation was the 1929 massacre of Haitian protestors by U.S. marines at Aux Cayes. This event shocked and angered many people, who not only expressed sympathy for Haitians but also interpreted the event within a global framework that encompassed the entire African Diaspora.

This chapter follows the transformation of black perceptions of Haiti and the black diaspora by investigating how the Aux Cayes crisis was understood in black public discourse. I contend that black Americans perceived U.S. policy in the Caribbean as fundamentally colonial, violent, and motivated by racial hatred. This articulation of foreign policy and racism understood racial violence as global, providing ground for black American sympathy with Haiti and a new interpretation of the African Diaspora. Furthermore, this interpretation departed from previous black appreciations of Haiti and the African Diaspora that functioned existentially and created community through shared metaphysical substance. Responding to the crisis at Aux Cayes, black Americans interpreted the African Diaspora in *political* terms, and that shift created new opportunities for reflexive commentary within the black community in the United States.

U.S. Imperialism in the Caribbean

Haiti occupies the western third of the island of San Domingo. Haitian culture is particular on the island, differing from that of its eastern neighbor, the Dominican Republic, because each aspect of the island has, in its own way, retained elements of its French and Spanish colonial legacy respectively. Throughout its history as an independent state, Haiti has maintained volatile relationships with foreign powers; its governments have restricted foreign ownership of Haitian land and severely regulated foreign investment and trade. The history of European and U.S. policy in the Caribbean is often explained as an effort to overcome this protectionist tradition and open up Haitian markets to Western capital. In the early years of the twentieth century, European and U.S. governments explored various measures to increase their influence in the Caribbean. Because public opinion in the United States did not support "empire building," the U.S. government justified its interventions in South America and the Caribbean basin as "counter-imperial" measures intended to protect defenseless nations from European expansion. In 1904 President Roosevelt issued the "Roosevelt Corollary" to the Monroe Doctrine in order to retard extrahemispheric influence in Caribbean affairs. He placed Dominican customhouses under receivership and took control of Dominican payments of its foreign debt. The Roosevelt Corollary assumed that economic intervention in Caribbean affairs was neither imperial nor colonial; it would, instead, provide stability to the region by "protecting" it from the exploitative European powers.

Roosevelt's successor, President Taft, expanded this policy through economic relationships and by encouraging U.S. banks to loan money to struggling island governments. On the one hand, the government's policies seemed destined to help develop the Caribbean: the State Department facilitated connections between U.S. capital and Caribbean leaders. At the same time, however, this "help" allowed U.S. banks to impose steep interest rates on Caribbean governments that accepted their assistance. During Taft's presidency, the increased involvement of the State Department and declining cooperation with international banking interests caused U.S. loans to the Caribbean to take on more pronounced nationalist dimensions.

In 1913, newly elected President Wilson delivered an address at the Southern Commercial Congress in Mobile, Alabama. In this speech he outlined his position toward Latin America, South America, and the Caribbean. The president suggested that the United States' colonial occupation and the influence of Europe in the Western hemisphere provided a common ground among the countries in these areas and concluded that this shared experience with colonialism warranted U.S. mediation of political disputes and military intervention in these countries. Ironically, Wilson's argument implied that the most efficient path to political independence and stability for emerging governments was to recognize and capitulate to the hegemony of the United States throughout the Western hemisphere.[4] This speech is a demonstration of how U.S. policy in the Caribbean during this period was justified using the language of the Progressive Era. Wilson correlated political instability with corruption and suggested that domestic unrest was a tool of European imperialism.[5] Thus, for him, a moral imperative sanctioned aggressive U.S. intervention in unstable states. In his eyes, such intervention was necessary to cleanse the political cultures of these nations of internal and external threats to efficient, self-sufficient governance.

From 1908 to 1915, Haiti experienced a series of brief presidential tenures, each established and then violently overthrown. In 1915, President Guillermo Sam attempted to hold onto power by jailing his political adversaries and their relatives. In July he was ousted and his body publicly mutilated. Citing the need to quell this unrest, protect the Panama Canal, and secure economic interests in Haiti, President Wilson ordered the invasion and occupation of the country. In 1917 the U.S. government legitimated its invasion by a treaty, but soon after its passage the United States forced the dissolution of Haiti's congress because its members refused to allow foreign ownership of land. In its place, the United States established a puppet government that ratified a new constitution authored by Secretary of the Navy Franklin Delano Roosevelt.[6] In the early stages of the occupation, violent conflict between Haitians and U.S. marines was not unusual. Haitian independence fighters, known as *"cacos,"* organized resistance from rural areas. However, by 1919 the U.S. marines had quelled the violence and established centralized control.

The occupation of Haiti represented a significant moment in the development of U.S. foreign policy because it deviated from nineteenth-century modes of European imperialism, ushering in the so-called Good Neighbor Policy that drove U.S. foreign policy in the Caribbean for much of the twentieth century. Unlike the European powers, in this new mode the United States experimented with alternatives to outright military conquest—a treaty-sanctioned occupation, partnership with puppet governments, and coercion and censorship—to establish and maintain social control. These policies limited access to information about the tenor and effects of U.S. policies in Haiti and obscured the imperial dimensions of the occupation, especially those interests fueled by the economic agendas of powerful U.S. banks.

Nevertheless, although economic and political concerns undoubtedly motivated U.S. policy, analysis of those ambitions alone is inadequate to understanding U.S. policy in the Caribbean during this period. The U.S. occupation of Haiti occurred in a context in which "Haiti" was already laden with colonial assumptions about the periphery of modernity. Mary Renda, one of many cultural theorists working in the tradition inspired by Edward Said's *Orientalism,* argues that American culture viewed Haiti through the lenses of gendered, paternalist codes that made the occupation seem not only prudent but imperative. These codes feminized Haiti, suggesting that it was chaotic, unstable, and dependent on the custodianship of a rational, masculine authority. In this context, U.S. occupation was necessary in order to maintain American masculinity, and failure to fulfill this obligation implied the failure of social structures fundamental to the integrity of the American nation. Renda's investigation of how contemporary gender stereotypes figured in the occupation of Haiti is insightful, but it underemphasizes the equally significant role played by colonial discourse about race in the adoption and administration of the occupation. The subordination of the racial dimensions of the occupation is problematic, because it overlooks how upheavals in Haiti and its subsequent occupation had distinct resonances for European Americans and black Americans.[7]

Occupying Haiti

The occupation was a significant economic and foreign policy issue, but it also had implications for domestic racial politics and rhetoric; race was a central component of the discursive context in which U.S. policies were formed. The U.S. occupation of Haiti emerged from and reinforced the ideology of American white supremacy, and it inspired a specific rhetoric in black America. For many Euro-Americans, intervention in Haiti was a step toward the solution of the "Negro problem" back home, and whites viewed Haitians of all classes and hues as indistinguishable from the U.S. blacks they "knew" in the American South. Colonel Littleton Walker, who served in Haiti in the early years of the occupation, stated that the Haitians "are niggers in spite of the thin varnish of education and refinement."[8] Secretary of State Robert Lansing averred that Haitians shared an "inherent tendency to revert to savagery" with Afro-Americans and Liberians. Lansing complained that this tendency made the United States' "negro problem practically unsolvable."[9]

In Haiti, U.S. marines enforced Jim Crow policies that established separate public spaces. In particular, these policies focused on social clubs and hotels frequented by Haiti's mulatto aristocracy. That aristocracy represented a mixture of racial ambiguity and European civilization that threatened the plausibility of simple racial dichotomies and the possibility of "white" cultural purity. In the United States, B. Baringer claimed that black American immigration to Haiti offered a logical solution to international and domestic political exigencies. In 1916 he pleaded with President Wilson for mass emigration of black Americans to occupied Haiti. For example, Baringer argued that a population shift would lessen the insidious threat to white women posed by the enduring presence of black men in the South. He wrote that, "in the past thirty years there has been a great improvement in the rural south . . . in every line, with one ominous exception. There is no improvement in the safety of the white woman of the rural sections. . . . The very children amongst the coming generation of negroes are now yielding to this sexual obsession."[10] However, arguments like this in favor of U.S. black emigration to Haiti assumed American homogeneity. Euro-America and the African Diaspora were considered distinct cultural spaces, and the danger of intermixture seen as controllable if the African population were localized and contained in one space.

President Wilson did, in fact, encourage U.S. blacks to move to Haiti, as did many black American emigration organizations; as a result, emigration to Haiti increased substantially from 1915 to 1920. At the same time, however, immigration *from* Haiti increased as well. Between 1910 and 1920 nearly five thousand people from the Caribbean immigrated to the United States every year.[11] Although the majority of this population originated in the British West Indies, many were also from Haiti. In the 1920s the Haitian and French West Indian presence in New York City's black communities was significant enough to warrant a full page in Marcus Garvey's *Negro World* that was written in French by Theodora Holly, daughter of the nineteenth-century emigrationist. Haiti's traditional significance in black American history, the racist rhetoric and policies of the occupation, and the increasingly multinational composition of African American urban centers all made the occupation a pressing public issue in black American communities.

In the early years of the occupation, black America's response to the occupation was diffuse and acknowledged little intimacy with Haiti. In one of the earliest black American responses to the U.S. invasion, Booker T. Washington editorialized that the United States was being "compelled to control matters largely because of the fault of the Haitians." Haitians, according to Washington, were a "backward people in need of discipline and enlightenment," and Haitian incompetence made U.S. intervention imperative. Washington defended the U.S. government, saying that the government "found it necessary to take a hand in the affairs of Haiti" or "permit others to do so."[12]

A few editorials by black Americans in newspapers like the *Afro-American Ledger,* the *Boston Guardian,* the *Philadelphia Ledger,* and the *New York Age* mentioned the occupation as a matter of concern, but they treated the U.S. action solely as an issue of foreign policy. The black national papers like the *Chicago Defender* and *Pittsburgh Courier* rarely mentioned the occupation of Haiti at all. From 1916 to 1920 their editorial sections were completely devoid of comment on the island or its occupation. This silence can be partially explained by the official suppression of information from Haiti exerted by the occupying forces and the chilling effects of the Espionage Act of 1917 and the Sedition Act of 1918 that likely inhibited critical editorials about the occupation. Moreover, during this period dominated by the First World War speaking out against the occupation was rhetorically problematic, as it conflicted with the growing sense of patriotism felt by many Americans, black and white alike. Still, despite these issues, the infrequency of comment on Haiti by the black press even after the conclusion of the war suggests that the occupation was not yet, by and large, a pressing local concern in black America.

So, it was not until the late teens and early 1920s that black newspapers began to speak out against the racist dimensions of U.S. policy in Haiti. In the most extreme examples, increasing black militancy and violent marine suppression of Haitian unrest inspired black newspapers to celebrate "the Haitian revolutionaries as freedom fighters in the tradition of African American abolitionists such as Gabriel Prosser, Denmark Vesey, and Nat Turner."[13] At the other end of the spectrum, the *Chicago Defender* and the *Pittsburgh Courier* began to discuss the occupation, but still relegated their coverage to less prominent pages and refrained from arguing a position on the occupation. Most of the black press lay somewhere in the vast middle ground; they ran editorials and articles defending the Haitian people against claims of their inferiority, but they rarely criticized the actions of the federal government directly.[14]

The *Negro World* was one of the few black papers that consistently covered the occupation; however, even Garvey's Black Nationalist newspaper exhibited ambivalence about the occupation. In February and March of 1921 The *World* published articles by Haitians who attempted to correct misconceptions about the occupation and to combat prejudices about the Haitian people. An anonymous open letter to President-elect

Harding published on February 26 decried the "cruelties and abuses" visited on the people of Haiti and Santo Domingo by the "U.S. drunken marines." The author then went on to state that he did not wish Uncle Sam to "meddle in the internal affairs of any other nation."[15] On the other hand, the March 3 *Negro World* published an essay by two "Delegates of the Haitian People," Perceval Thoby and Steino Vincent. This editorial countered public assertions about the "moral and intellectual" conditions in Haiti by arguing that its Catholic churches and schools were well-organized. In addition, the authors praised the occupation for maintaining free speech and a free press and for protecting the common Haitian from the "autocratic military despotism" of prior regimes.[16]

James Weldon Johnson toured Haiti in 1920 under the auspices of *The Nation*. He then published a series of articles generated by his research and experience. The series, entitled "Self-Determining Haiti," challenged derogatory assumptions about Haiti by lauding its "100 years of self government and liberty"[17] and, through its lionizing of Haitian revolutionary King Henri Christophe, asserted a proud and independent Haitian patrimony.[18] Johnson's rhetoric was fundamentally recuperative and an effort to cleanse his audience of racist assumptions about Haiti. Indeed, he even claimed that Haitians were an "exceptionally clean people" who "use more soap per capita that any country in the world."[19]

In 1922 Johnson argued that the NAACP should not take too public a role in the anti-occupation lobby, because it would not "do the Haitians' cause much good to for it to be found out that the movement behind it was entirely Negro."[20] He was aware of the effect that seemingly Black Nationalist appeals might have on sympathy for the Haitian cause. In these early years of the occupation, Johnson acknowledged that the connection between black America and Haiti was more symbolic than political. Moreover, he was aware that, although African Americans might despise the racist language used by some against native Haitians, they were far from univocal on the issue of the occupation. In December 1923 he wrote to Haitian nationalist Joseph Mirault expressing pessimism about the success of a sustained fund-raising program in African American newspapers.[21] The occupation had become stable and bureaucratic and thus warranted a shift in political energies.

Although Haiti received very little attention in public argument during the mid-twenties, many black American organizations did show support for the Haitian people by soliciting and supplying resources to improve their quality of life under the occupation. The Overseas Navi-gation and Overseas Trading Company, founded in 1922 and underwrit-ten by black American banks, facilitated trade between U.S. and Haitian ports, and Mary McLeod Bethune served on the advisory committee of a black women's club that held clothing drives for needy Haitian children. These organizations directed public sympathies for Haiti and relied heav-ily on the contributions of expatriates.[22]

During the mid-1920s, the occupation received little coverage in black newspapers, but at the close of the decade violent conflict between U.S. marines and a group of unarmed Haitian protestors inspired a dramatic increase in the frequency, passion, and focus of black American interpre-tations of the occupation.[23] Unlike the earlier commentary found in vari-ous editorials, this new wave of attention not only condemned racism, it implicated the actions of the U.S. government in that racism.

The protest began in early 1929 as a student strike. The occupation government in Haiti had supplied ten thousand dollars to students at the agricultural teachers training college at Damien in Southern Haiti. Many of the recipients were bourgeois students who used the money to pay local peasants to do their manual labor. In the fall of 1929 the gov-ernment decreased the subsidy by 20 percent, making it more difficult for the students to hire others to perform their tasks. Affected students protested and won the support of law and medical students throughout the country, yet even with this additional help, the strike had to struggle to gain momentum until December. On December 6 at the port of Aux Cayes, fifteen hundred farmers and peasants, overburdened by laws that benefited only larger farms and corporate producers, marched to the Aux Cayes customhouse to present a list of complaints. The crowd of protes-tors was met by twenty U.S. marines who, intimidated by the size of the crowd and unable to communicate with them in French, opened fire. U.S. news agencies reported that anywhere from five to twenty-five Haitians were killed and at least seventy-five wounded.[24]

This event was the catalyst that changed how the black community in the United States talked about the U.S. occupation. Although black papers had, on rare occasions, criticized the occupation, up to then the vast majority of the black press had not portrayed the U.S. government as an entity complicit in the racism directed toward Haiti. Now, because of the Aux Cayes incident, that changed. Oscar De Priest, the first black congressman since Reconstruction, gave his first speech to the House of

Representatives on the crisis at Aux Cayes. He claimed that he was "carrying out the wishes of the people identified with my racial group all over this country," because he had "received hundreds of telegrams" from black people imploring him to take a stand on the issue.[25] Haiti also dominated the front pages of the major black national newspapers — the *Chicago Defender,* the *Pittsburgh Courier,* and the *New York Amsterdam News.* From December 1929 through January 1930 black newspapers covered the occupation extensively, and the back pages of these papers were saturated with editorials and letters from readers who debated the significance of the Aux Cayes massacre and the actions of the U.S. government.

Interpreting the Occupation after Aux Cayes

Days after the shooting at Aux Cayes, the front page of the *New York Amsterdam News* declared, "from the meager and garbled reports of the white press we learn that Haiti has risen in revolt."[26] This report was significant because it acknowledged from the very beginning that the crisis in Haiti was a "political" event. Furthermore, the article expressed skepticism about the likelihood of reliable reporting in the "white" press. Indeed, the black press interpreted the fact that Euro-Americans appeared to treat the event casually as suggesting that racism might be preventing a full account of the incident; therefore, an alternative venue, a second source of information, was necessary through which to interpret the loss of Haitian life. The black press provided a forum in which to investigate the more specific details of the conflict and, equally important, a space to interpret and debate these facts — in essence, to create a meaning for the event in black America.[27]

After the violence at Aux Cayes, black American newspapers received letters to the editor that identified the occupation as a colonial endeavor; indeed, many letters described the occupation by explicitly relating it to European colonialism. For example, on December 28, 1929, the *Chicago Defender,* in its "Other Papers Say" section, published the following excerpt from a story in the *St. Louis Post-Dispatch:* "In July, 1915, when our sense of proportion was distorted, perhaps, by the World war, we bowed to the logic of events, we sent our marines to end a reign of terror, we took on the manifold duties as inventoried in 'The White Man's Burden' of Kipling, and we are still there. But peace and tranquility are not there."[28] This letter placed U.S. policies in the context of European expansionism, implicitly denying that the occupation served legitimate political ends (as it arose from a state of disorientation), or that it represented the fulfillment of a particularly "American" destiny or responsibility. In fact the occupation was a political consideration that should be judged, not according to the ideals of a manifest destiny, but according to the practical and prudent considerations of its immediate purpose and outcome. According to this letter and others like it, the occupation was a failure, because it was unnecessary to promote the nation's self-defense. Furthermore, although the U.S. government had justified the occupation by claiming that it would benefit Haitians, in reality the country's continuing unrest demonstrated how it had failed to meets its own attested goal. The violence at Aux Cayes was proof that the occupation had failed.

Other writers also interpreted the occupation as colonial but were even less forgiving. An editorial published in the *New York Amsterdam News* argued that, "like Banquo's ghost, the Haitian question will not go away. . . . Though buried under volumes of official reports of American benefits to Haiti—order established, roads built, public works undertaken, great loans secured from Wall Street and other de-odorizers—the rottenness of the American occupation of Haiti still sends forth its stench."[29] Kelly Miller's argument acknowledged the occupation's humanitarian intentions and its benefits to Haitian infrastructure, but it viewed these accomplishments as incidental to the occupation's spirit and administration, which were fundamentally corrupt. Despite its few progressive accomplishments, the occupation was tainted by the avarice at its base. As an editorial in the *Pittsburgh Courier* lamented, "There is not the slightest reason for remaining in the country any longer, except to exploit it for the benefit for American bankers."[30]

This rhetoric stripped away the patina of benign paternalism that had been used to justify the occupation and, in the process, called into question one of the most important dimensions of diffusionist thought. As I discussed earlier, colonial discourse was grounded in the belief in a differentiation between distinct cultural spaces—the center and the periphery—and it assumed that the metropole, the center, was justified in how it policed the exchange between itself and the periphery because it was acting in the periphery's best interest. That is, the colonizer was making a sacrifice that benefited the colony to an extent greater than the benefits experienced by the colonial power. During the occupation of Haiti, these discursive characteristics were readily apparent; apologists for the occupation characterized Haiti as childlike — namely, dependent on the policies, structure, and discipline the United States was providing its immature island neighbor. One excellent example of this rhetoric is evident in the pages of the *National Geographic,* which, throughout the late teens depicted Haiti as a diminutive "orphan" that required the guidance of Euro-America.[31] After the violence at Aux Cayes, editorials in black newspapers began to question the logic of paternalism used by those who supported the occupation. More to the point, these writers specifically identified the United States as a colonial power that was exploiting and repressing the Haitian people for its own benefit.

The key to the new consciousness within the black community seemed to be the particular variety of violence exerted by the U.S. military. Days after the conflict at Aux Cayes, the front page of the *Chicago Defender* declared that "the United States marines have massacred more Haitians. They have shot unarmed natives down as they would do so many cattle, and have left the dead and wounded strewing the fields of Cayes."[32] Another interpretation of the crisis highlighted the violence, but it also compared the violence in Haiti with historical instances of violence that comprised U.S. history, claiming that "the Boston massacre was a tiny thing compared to the Haitian massacre. The colonists were not bullied and insulted by the troops of a foreign power. In fact, the colonists themselves did the insulting. Compared with the conduct of the United States marines in Haiti, the British troops in Boston were models of decorum."[33] In this register, the violence that characterized the occupation was too capricious, too uncivil, to serve political ends. Indeed, not only was the violence at Aux Cayes described as contrary to reasonable political goals, the black press interpreted the act as representative of white supremacy in the United States.

The true significance of black criticism of the U.S. government was not its condemnation of unwarranted violence, however, but the fact that this criticism involved an association between the experiences of Haitians and the experiences of black Americans. According to one writer, "the slaveholders of America, too, built roads and bridges, but that did not justify slavery. The ancient Egyptian kings built colossal pyramids with slave labor, but were those tremendous piles worth the suffering of the thousands who raised them?"[34] This passage is instructive, because it suggests a possible ground for common experience in the African Diaspora. Mentioning slavery in both America and Egypt, it combines the recent history of the new world with the ancient history of Africa to suggest an experience of exploitation exclusive to present and past members of the African Diaspora. Thus the anticolonial sentiment expressed in interpretations of the U.S. occupation of Haiti was not merely anti-imperial; it also understood the occupation as a product of the racial assumptions that underwrote the politics of colonialism. Colonialism had created a set of racially coded differences that inspired the occupation but also allowed black Americans to perceive a connection to the African Diaspora.

A number of editorials published in black newspapers accused the occupation of *creating* racial division. In an editorial in the *New York Amsterdam News,* Joel A. Rogers opined that the American invasion had "created additional hates and factions that are only waiting for the withdrawal of the marines to break out like so many new boils."[35] A month later an editorial in the same paper asserted that the potential for conflict created by the marines was racial, "not because of its nature, but because the marines have made it so. They have not used the word Papist; but they have made the island ring with the word 'nigger.' "[36] An editorial in the *New York Amsterdam News* asked if "the marines conducted themselves like policemen, or like a southern mob" and stated that, although they were "sent to teach law and order, they have behaved like lynchers."[37] The *Chicago Defender* reported that "Representative Henry Huddleston is reported to have said it was fortunate that no American marines had been killed [at Aux Cayes], as he would not give the life of a marine for the whole country of Haiti. In other words the life of a white American in Haiti is worth more than the whole population whose color is in contrast to the pale faces of the southern crackers."[38]

After the crisis at Aux Cayes, many people of African descent interpreted the occupation of Haiti as a dangerous extension of the racial politics of the American South into a space previously devoid of such racial divisions. The occupation itself became evidence of Euro-America's contempt for the entire African Diaspora and for black people around the globe, and the violence in Haiti convinced many black Americans that it was "men imbued with the idea that black men were born to be trampled by white men who have brought about the present state of affairs."[39] Indeed, for a good number of black Americans, the situation in Haiti demonstrated that the putatively humanitarian policies of white governments that intervened to help black countries were not benign; rather, they were complicit with attitudes and actions of domestic racism. This articulation of foreign policy portrayed racial violence as a global phenomenon; even people outside of U.S. borders could experience "American"-style racial violence. By viewing the violence at Aux Cayes as the result of exploitative colonial policies inflicted upon a similarly "raced" people, black American interpretations of the crisis were also interpretations of the African Diaspora as a political condition.

Interpreting the African Diaspora

Kelly Miller explicitly acknowledged the implications of the crisis at Aux Cayes for domestic politics when he editorialized in the *New York Amsterdam News:* "this incident ought to serve to bring the American Negro to his political sense."[40] Other editorials in black periodicals expressed a similar understanding of the occupation of Haiti and pointed to a direction for this "political sense," suggesting that it could be a frame of reference through which African Americans might challenge the institutions of U.S. democracy. In these articles, the African Diaspora became a source of black American political authority.

Articles published in black American periodicals interpreted the United States' policies in Haiti as evidence of the failure of U.S. political institutions, locally and internationally. Haitian Dantes Belegrande, in a 1930 article published in *Opportunity* and translated by J. A. Rogers, argued that the political instability in Haiti that had served as a warrant for the invasion was also present in the United States:

> So also are many of the courts in the United States, particularly in the South where it is impossible for Negroes to get justice when one of the litigants is white. And yet there is no talk of declaring martial law in Florida, Mississippi, South Carolina, or Arkansas. The Haitians go on strike, throw a few ink bottles, club a couple of officers and martial law is declared; the southerners Jim Crow negroes, hold them in peonage, tax them without representation, lynch them when "biggety" and these evils go practically unnoticed.[41]

These statements are remarkable in two ways. First, citing American policy in Haiti as a point of reference, Belegrande indicts the institutions responsible for maintaining justice *inside* the United States. Indeed, Belegrande suggests that the institutions of American democracy, the justice system and the state in general, are incapable of administering democracy.

Second, the text argues that U.S. foreign policy is ineffectual and misdirected. Thus Belegrande critiques the institutions of U.S. democracy in both domestic and international contexts.

In a similar vein, an editorial in the *Chicago Defender* argued that American foreign policy distracted American institutions from fulfilling their mandate to promote and protect democracy in the United States. U.S. marines, it suggested, "would have no time to run to Haiti and Nicaragua if they devoted some effort to cleaning up conditions at home. There is more disrespect for the laws of this country per square foot of Mississippi and other southern states than there is in the whole of Haiti."[42] The United States' failure to implement democratic rights at home and abroad was proof of the impotence of the institutions of American democracy.

In many ways, this institutional criticism was not new. Racial progressives in the United States often argued against the hypocrisy of American racial politics and the inability of the institutions of U.S. democracy to ensure democracy. Moreover, U.S. policy in Cuba was greeted by a similar anticolonial critique in black newspapers in 1898. What is interesting in this case, however, is how this critique was placed in an international context, employing foreign conditions and even foreign policy as a frame of reference. Throughout the nineteenth century Frederick Douglass had lambasted the hypocrisy of the United States; nevertheless, Douglass's sense of democracy was thoroughly implicated in narratives of American exceptionalism. His rhetoric, like much of the rhetoric of revolution, was concerned with the particularly American rights of U.S. citizens.[43] Likewise, Ida B. Wells-Barnett criticized the United States justice system, but her analysis, like Douglass's, argued for the extension of citizenship rights to all Americans within the country's borders.

First, Belegrande's argument differs in that his analysis finds fault not solely in the disposition of American justice for American citizens but in the fact that U.S. action was similarly racist both in the United States and throughout the globe. This conjunction of American foreign and domestic policy suggests that black Americans and Haitians suffered from a similar political condition. In a context where political protest involved national and international components, a new identity — an international identity based on a common political agenda — became not only possible but desirable.

Second, interpretation of the crisis at Aux Cayes implied that black America's intimacy with the African Diaspora was a warrant for political authority. Perhaps the clearest example of this development appears in the debate over how to constitute an investigative committee. Fallout from the Aux Cayes rebellion led to President Hoover's quick appointment of a committee to investigate and adjudicate the occupation in Haiti.[44] Black American newspapers vociferously debated how race should matter in the selection of a U.S. representative to Haiti. Kelly Miller noted, "the mind of the Afro-American is much agitated over the complexion of the commission."[45]

U.S. diplomatic representation to Haiti had symbolic importance to black America; for Haiti was one of the first theaters of foreign policy in which black Americans played a substantial role. In 1869, President Grant had appointed the first black American to represent the United States, Ebenezer Don Carlos Basset, who served as minister resident and consul general to Haiti. After his tenure, the minister to Haiti was traditionally a black position.[46] The association of the Haitian post with African Americans was so strong that even Grover Cleveland appointed an African American to serve, John Edward West Thompson, the first black Democrat to be appointed to the Foreign Service. In the second decade of the twentieth century, President Wilson limited black American participation in government and foreign policy. In 1913 he resegregated federal work forces, and in 1916, he fired the incumbent minister to Haiti, appointing the first white American to serve in this capacity since the inception of the position.[47] In 1924, the Hoover administration standardized selection for Foreign Service employment, ostensibly creating a merit-based procedure; nevertheless, the process required an interview that was often used to eliminate black Americans from the pool of qualified applicants.[48]

The *Pittsburgh Courier,* the *Chicago Defender,* and the *New York Amsterdam News* devoted considerable print space to arguing the relative merits of prominent African Americans to serve on Hoover's commission. W. E. B. Du Bois, James Weldon Johnson, and Oscar De Priest were discussed as possible representatives. An editorial in the *New York Amsterdam News* opined that, because of the delicate circumstances involved in the Haitian situation: "it now seems that the placement of a Negro representative on the commission would best promote the accomplishment of the great end in view. It would the more easily compose the just sensibilities of the Haitians to see one of their own clime and degree entrusted with high governmental functions."[49] From this perspective, intimacy with the

African Diaspora translated into a practical contribution to foreign policy and the resolution of those political issues which were inherent to the occupation. Black America's racial connection with Haiti was a crucial factor in the political calculus of this foreign policy situation.

Some commentators on the occupation extrapolated the political warrant implied by the situation in Haiti to a general claim about African American agency in future foreign and domestic policy issues. For example, George Little of Pennsylvania wrote a letter to the editor of the *Chicago Defender* in which he argued that, in general, "the United States should deal with colored nations through her colored citizens."[50] Claims like this implied there was a connection between African Americans and the Diaspora, but they also did not deny black America's primary citizenship. Rather, affiliation with the African international community provided the foundation for black America's particular contribution to the administration of U.S. democracy and provided opportunity for black America to voice its opinion in policy debates. Perhaps most important, the political affiliation between the Diaspora and the United States created an opportunity for black Americans to situate themselves within narratives that fused American identity and foreign policy. Little continued, arguing: "If the United States wants to stabilize Latin American countries, why not send down her black citizens? The ugly and ever present problem of race prejudice would no longer exist. Such a move would provide an outlet for our youth who could be employed in this great work. The United States could establish a black empire throughout Latin America through the agency of her own black citizens."[51] In this case, the language and policies of empire allowed the author to accentuate both African and American dimensions of his ethos.

Thus, the interpretations of the crisis at Aux Cayes implied black political agency at the intersection of the African Diaspora and the institutions of American democracy. However, the language of empire also testified to the complexity of how black Americans interpreted the Diaspora in 1929. Although the rhetorical response to the massacre at Aux Cayes expressed more political intimacy between U.S. black Americans and Haitians, it also retained subtle distinctions between these populations and between middle-class and proletarian components of the political community. For example, George Little also lamented that it was "regrettable that the virus of American civilization could not be injected into Haiti at the point of a bayonet . . . the proper degree of

civility will not be maintained by these savages."[52] Little's remarks illustrate the complexity of the interpretation of the African Diaspora that
emerged from the U.S. occupation of Haiti; it did undermine the diffusionist assumptions of colonial discourse, but it did not abolish their
presence, even within the black community.

Perhaps the clearest evidence of this tendency is found in W. E. B. Du
Bois's evolving response to the occupation. In a letter to President Wilson dated August 3, 1915, Du Bois expressed concerns about the invasion:
"Hayti [*sic*] is not all bad. She has contributed something to human uplift
and if she has a chance she can do more ... it is not only our privilege as
a nation to rescue her from her worst self, but this would be in a sense a
solemn act of reparation on our part for the great wrongs afflicted by this
land on the negro race."[53] As the occupation progressed, Du Bois became
increasingly critical of its administration, but he continued to maintain
both this paternal posture *and* his awareness of the political implications
of the occupation for African America.

In 1929 Raymond L. Buell wrote to Du Bois asking for information
on Haiti and Du Bois's personal position on the occupation. Du Bois
responded by suggesting a policy. He proposed that the United States
"ought to send to Haiti civilian helpers in every line of education and
social uplift. Especially we ought to stop the beginning of the land mo-
nopoly and exploitation and restore to their rightful leadership the educated class of Haiti with every effort to induce them through example and
advice to lead a movement for the uplift of the masses."[54]

Du Bois's prescription for Haiti clearly resonates with the diffusionist
paradigm. Despite his growing dissatisfaction with the occupation and
its administration — Du Bois had been a vocal critic of the exploitative
policies of U.S. marines since the early 1920s — his remedy for the crisis
perpetuated the ideological assumptions that had justified the occupation
over a decade before. Still, as reported in the *New York Times,* after the
crisis at Aux Cayes, Du Bois participated in a public debate at the Hotel
Astor in New York City. During that debate, he defended Haiti's democratic history and blamed the United States for "making the country less
democratic than it had been in a thousand years."[55] Of particular importance to this study is the fact that Du Bois used this opportunity to rail
against the American South. In his mind, the problems in Haiti and the
problems at home were clearly connected, because both were evidence of
a fundamental failure of American political institutions. The racial hatred

so evident in the South had become a problem in the administration of U.S. foreign policy.

Du Bois's understanding of the occupation of Haiti illustrates how U.S. black America's identification with that country relied on the reification of ontological difference rather than achieving community in spite of it; Haiti's distance from modern civilization and political power were important components of this diasporic bond. Although Du Bois recognized the intersecting interests of black America and Haiti due to their common political condition, he still perceived that each party had distinct responsibilities and that those responsibilities correlated directly to essential differences between Haitians and black Americans. Still, the change in Du Bois's views from 1916 to 1929 was significant. Like other members of the black community, the violence in Haiti provided a context in which black Americans could criticize American democracy from a reconfigured position within the international scene of the African Diaspora. Thus, despite the continuing presence of the diffusionist paradigm based in difference, the shift from an existential affinity between black America and the African Diaspora to a political similarity between them had progressive ramifications.

The bald aggression of American colonialism in the Caribbean encouraged black America to reexamine its relationship to colonialism and U.S. democracy. Many black Americans interpreted the massacre at Aux Cayes as the culmination of a violent colonial policy motivated by racial hatred. In turn, they sympathized with Haiti's people, who also appeared to be suffering from the same kind of racial violence that black Americans experienced in the United States. Ultimately, this sympathy led to the expression of a limited political solidarity in black newspapers and periodicals. Meanwhile, in Haiti the occupation unified disparate economic classes and racial types in pursuit of the goal of political independence. As U.S. marines enacted Jim Crow doctrine, closing Haitian businesses and patronizing only segregated establishments, Haitians used U.S. racism to reexamine rifts in their own culture.

Haiti, like many formerly colonized West Indian islands, maintained a caste system based on color and class; "Mulatto Haitians" retained most of the island's power and wealth. In the face of U.S. aggression, Haitians from disparate communities and social and economic backgrounds reconfigured the meaning of Haitian identity and built political and economic connections between once clashing elements of Haitian society.

The occupation had a similar unifying effect in black America. Groups that had once been at odds agreed in their opposition to the occupation. Even James Weldon Johnson, a noted critic of Marcus Garvey, corresponded with the head of the UNIA in order to coordinate opposition to the U.S. occupation.

Early in 1930, the Hoover administration acquiesced to pressure from the president of Haiti and to European Americans, declining to appoint a black person to the committee investigating the occupation of Haiti.[56] Eventually, Hoover appointed a secondary commission to report on the Haitian educational system, and African American Robert Russa Moton, inheritor of Booker T. Washington's mantle at Tuskeegee, chaired this subordinate commission. In 1930 Moton and his delegation of African American dignitaries returned from their official visit to Haiti on a steamship. Despite their status as representatives of the president of the United States, a group of Euro-American passengers asked the diplomats to entertain the steamship passengers by singing some Negro spirituals. Moton and the diplomats complied with the insulting request.

News of Moton's foray into entertainment infuriated black journalist George S. Schuyler, and he denounced the commission as group of "Uncle Toms." Curiously, Schuyler also attacked the spirituals themselves for being "counterrevolutionary." He claimed: "Negroes are engaged and have been for a long time in a bitter war for a place in this civilization as full fledged men and women. That which comforts and pleases the enemy can not be beneficial. . . . [W]e are a great army moving forward to better things — a larger share of this world's goods and pleasures here and now, not when we die and roost on celestial banisters. The true soldier thinks of victory on terra firma and not 'pie in the sky, bye and bye.'"[57] Schuyler's stinging criticism of Moton and his skepticism about the utility of black folk tradition seem at odds: How could he indict Moton as an Uncle Tom while he ridiculed the possibility of authentic blackness? The answer lies in Schuyler's own evolving appreciation of the role of the Africa Diaspora in black American identity as he turned his critical eye to the nation of Liberia in 1931.

CHAPTER 4

"Modern" Slaves

The Liberian Labor Crisis and the Politics of Race and Class

T HE VIOLENCE AT AUX CAYES inspired the United States to initiate a policy called "Haitianzation," which gradually ceded political power to Haitian authorities. The same violence encouraged people of African descent in the United States to question their relationships to Africa, its diaspora, and United States democracy. As the colonial policies of the occupation became public knowledge, black Americans recognized a common experience with racial violence and expressed sympathy for Haiti's people. In this sense, the U.S. occupation of Haiti and its accompanying racist violence increased the relevance of the African Diaspora to black ethos within the United States. That is, the way in which black people talked about their collective identity involved common political experiences that crossed state boundaries and geographic distance. Ultimately, the United States' colonial policies during its occupation of Haiti provided a political framework for understanding a truly international black diaspora that moved beyond racial heritage.

Despite an increase in political intimacy between black Americans and black "others," much of this rhetoric remained complicit with the assumptions of colonial discourse. Haiti and its culture remained exotic, and black Americans continued to insist that, despite the affinity that existed between themselves and Haitians, each occupied a separate place and had a distinct role to play in the fight against global racial violence. Alone, the perceptual changes that were transpiring within America's black communities were as yet insufficient to inspire a rhetoric free from the diffusionist logic of colonialism. However, as this chapter will now demonstrate, subsequent crises in the African Diaspora altered these perceptions even further and complicated the functions of both colonial discourse and the African Diaspora in black ethos.

In 1930, the League of Nations dispatched a committee headed by Britain's Dr. Cuthbert Christy to investigate reports of forced labor in Liberia. The "Christy Report" detailed the widespread practice of "pawning" Liberian children into indentured servitude to Americo-Liberian families, incidents of domestic slavery, abuses in the recruitment of labor to the island of Fernando Po, the use of the Liberian military to "motivate" laborers to build roads through the hinterland, and profiteering by some members of Americo-Liberian government. European nations used the report to justify past imperialist endeavors and to provide an imperative for further colonial encroachment into Africa. In the United States, the report was interpreted in the light of domestic racial politics. Racists argued that these problems proved that Liberia was a failed state and that this "failure" demonstrated the incapacity for self-government among populations of African descent.[1] For individuals who claimed a more "enlightened" stance with respect to race, the Liberian situation created a hermeneutic controversy and a rhetorical crisis. Black people living in the United States were particularly conflicted about the Christy Report and hotly debated the nature of Liberian "slavery." The core problem faced by black America was that the criticism leveled against the Americo-Liberian government seemed too similar to the derogatory appraisals of black political acumen in the African Diaspora; however, the charges of slavery and exploitation compelled empathy and, perhaps, support for indigenous Liberians. Furthermore, the symbolic importance of slavery as a moral issue, one with deep historical resonance, called for response. Arguments for solidarity with either native Liberians or the Americo-Liberian elite circulated in black communities.

Prominent black American journalist George S. Schuyler commented prolifically on the situation in Liberia. Schuyler had achieved public notoriety, partially through his arguments against affiliation of African Americans with Africa and his polemic assertion that the black American was a "lamp-blacked Anglo Saxon."[2] However, in the early 1930s Schuyler visited Liberia to investigate the Liberian labor crisis, and his experiences there inspired him to write a number of articles and a novel that portrayed the "reality" of the situation in Liberia and its significance for black people in diaspora.[3]

Schuyler's novel *Slaves Today: A Story of Liberia* was a fictional account of the plight of a Liberian laborer during the Liberian labor crisis of 1931. It was also the first novel by a black American set entirely in Africa and, according to Michael Peplow, the "first attempt at a realistic assessment of Africa by a black author."[4] The "realistic" character of the novel resulted from its journalistic and anthropological style; within its narrative, these empirical idioms were woven through literary forms that resembled the slave narrative and the character types of pulp fiction. Scholars in literary studies have cited this generic inconsistency as a source of the novel's artistic failure.[5] However, from a rhetorical perspective, the novel's articulation of the actual characteristics of an indigenous African culture within particularly "American" literary norms demonstrated a complex and innovative synthesis of the foreign and the familiar in the African Diaspora; indeed, the novel presented both a complex vision of Africa and a frame for empathy among diverse communities in the African Diaspora.

Although the Liberian labor crisis did not inspire grassroots activism in black America, Schuyler's novel expression of empathy with indigenous Liberians represents a significant development in the texture of black America's relationship to Africa. Indeed, *Slaves Today: A Story of Liberia* raises important questions about how expressions of diaspora have figured in African American rhetorical culture, how articulations of diasporic identity have confronted rhetorics of white supremacy, and how people of African descent living in the United States have participated in its foreign policy. In this sense, the novel provides a literary window into the politics of black identity in the early years of the Great Depression.

This chapter approaches *Slaves Today: A Story of Liberia* as a multifaceted rhetorical text—equal parts travelogue, documentary, political broadside, and work of fiction. I argue the text foregrounds the cultural particularity of native Liberians but also presents Liberian culture in a manner that resonates with experiences of Africans in diaspora; the novel illustrates how black workers around the globe endure the dehumanizing bureaucracies of the bourgeoisie and the imposition of racial thinking into their daily lives, both of which create static cultural spaces that deny the progressive potential of modernity. The novel's protagonist, Zo, embodies the ability to navigate the constraints of class and race and thus personifies the agency of an empowered African Diaspora. I conclude that the novel's construction of a Pan-African hero evinces an evolving black voice in the politics of white supremacy and the administration of U.S. foreign policy.

The Liberian Labor Crisis

Liberia was founded by the American Colonization Society in the early nineteenth century and was incorporated as a state by relocated populations from the African Diaspora in 1847. Throughout its history Liberia was, and still is, a space in which the native African population and Western cultures clash. Throughout its history, the country's economy has been the site of considerable conflict. For example, many of the early settlers to Africa, members of the Diaspora, engaged in trade rather than in the agricultural systems employed by the native population. Eventually, the Liberia of the nineteenth century was divided into two classes — a settler society that interacted with European traders and a native African population that produced many of the goods that were bought and sold by more recent immigrants. By the turn of the century, Liberia was a nation divided. Between ten and twelve thousand Americo-Liberians occupied an upper-class position and an indigenous population between fifteen hundred thousand and two million occupied a lower stratum. Impoverished by foreign loans and dependent on international trade, labor seemed to be Liberia's only stable economic resource.[6]

In 1914 Liberian president D. E. Howard signed a labor agreement with the governor-general of Spanish Guinea, which paid the Liberian government for each laborer shipped to Spanish cocoa plantations on the island of Fernando Po. It included provisions for worker safety and strict guidelines for terms of service. Workers' contracts were for one to two years, employers were approved by Liberian authorities, wages were paid in reliable British currency, and employment could not be extended beyond the period of the contract. From 1919 to 1926, 4,268 laborers were shipped to Fernando Po.[7]

World War I decreased the profitability of the labor agreement by increasing the cost of transporting workers. In 1918 the agreement was altered so that employers could extend contracts after the expiration of the initial two-year period. The alteration coincided with the circulation of rumors about worker abuse. Citing evidence of worker exploitation and the humanitarian warrant they implied, the Liberian government periodically restricted the flow of laborers to the island. These interdictions in the treaty also allowed the Liberian government to exercise its political authority and increase its profit, as the threat of a labor shortage could be used as leverage during negotiations. By the late 1920s, many Liberians were angry over the treatment of laborers shipped to Fernando Po and argued for an end to the agreement.[8] In 1927 Liberia's Secretary of State unilaterally terminated the 1914 accord.

Farmers on the island still needed laborers, and some Americo-Liberian private citizens with connections to the Liberian government still wanted to provide them; thus, in 1928 a group of farmers contracted with a group of Liberians to continue the labor trade privately. From 1928 to 1929, 2,431 workers were shipped to Fernando Po, and under this private agreement, worker exploitation increased: contracts were extended without worker consent, many workers were not paid, others contracted diseases and were not provided medical care or pay while ill. In June 1929 the United States intervened in Liberian labor practices, citing humanitarian grounds. In a letter to Liberian president Charles D. B. King, the U.S. minister to Liberia inquired about disturbing reports of the "export" of labor from the Liberian hinterland to Fernando Po and averred that the practice as reported was both "hardly distinguishable from organized slave trade" and was being carried out by the "services and influences of certain high government officials."[9] The letter disavowed any U.S. interest in the situation; nevertheless, U.S. capital was implicated in the decision to intervene in Liberia, because the continuation of the existing labor relationship conflicted with the ambitions of the Firestone Corporation. Firestone extended a number of loans to the Liberian government during the 1920s in order to gain access to Liberian rubber and the labor required to farm it. The private trade in Liberian labor competed with Firestone's access to workers and, more important, diluted its influence in Liberian politics.[10]

At the close of the 1920s, the Liberian labor policy was entangled in a web of competing colonial agendas and practices. This colonial endeavor, however, had specific implications for the African Diaspora. On its front page the New York Age proclaimed that "Freedmen" were both participants in and objects of exploitation.[11] Moreover, despite disavowal of colonial ambitions, U.S. policy echoed that of European imperialists. Thus, the situation in Liberia called for rhetoric that would identify the salient dimensions of the controversy, interrogate "American" colonial ambitions, and interpret a role for the African Diaspora relative to Liberian labor.

Liberian Labor in the African Diaspora

The controversy over Liberian "slave" labor was articulated through diverse configurations that assumed relationships between indigenous Liberian labor, black America, and modernity. Echoing their interpretation of the U.S. occupation of Haiti, many prominent black intellectuals expressed solidarity with the Americo-Liberian elite and held a paternal attitude toward indigenous Africa. In a series of "Post-scripts" in *The Crisis,* and later in an article entitled "Liberia, The League, and the United States" in *Foreign Affairs Magazine,* W. E. B. Du Bois argued that one could understand and judge Liberian labor practices only in the context of the global economy and the contest of civilizations.[12] In Du Bois's analysis, Liberia in general and Americo-Liberians in particular suffered from the racist policies of Western nations, and the attention paid to Liberian use of forced labor was yet another example of Western perfidy. Western capital had conspired to limit Liberian economic viability to such an extent that Americo-Liberians had no choice but to engage in labor practices that were not egalitarian; therefore, Western outrage was base, racist hypocrisy. From this perspective, Americo-Liberians were doing the best they could to make Liberia into a modern industrial nation. Du Bois's text described an African Diasporic community defined by the agency shared by the African American and Liberian elite. The laboring class of Liberians were absent from this collective identity, because it was largely a function of cultural proximity to a distinctly European modernity and, thus, distance from indigenous Liberia.

Du Bois implied that, when viewed through the appropriate historical perspective, Liberian "slavery" was similar to labor practices throughout the civilized world; labor in general and native Liberians in particular were resources to be developed in aid of a transatlantic modernity. Du Bois blamed Western imperialism for the existence of slavery in Liberia, but he also castigated Western racism for retarding the development of Americo-Liberian modernity. For example, he apologized for the system of pawning, calling it a "method by which native children are adopted into civilized Liberian families for education" and arguing that it has

"resulted in such widespread intermarriage between American Negroes
and native Liberians that the line between the two groups is almost fanciful." Du Bois also went to great pains to defend Americo-Liberian actions
in his redaction of the Christy Report. He erroneously argued that "Vice
President Yancy was flagrantly guilty, but Yancy was not an Americo-
Liberian but a native African tribesman, whose election to the Vice Presidency was especially hailed as a recognition of the native Africans in the
political organization of the Liberians."[13]

In the next issue of *The Crisis,* Charles S. Johnson, a member of the
Christy Commission, sympathetically critiqued Du Bois's problematic
description of Yancy's guilt, putative indigenousness, and democratic
progress in Liberia and corrected some of his facts. Johnson reminded
Du Bois and readers of *The Crisis* that Yancy was in fact an Americo-
Liberian, whose "elevation to the Vice Presidency was accomplished
against the wishes of the native population" and who remained in office
"over their protests, which have not been at any time very effective in
the political organization of the Liberians."[14] In his critique of Du Bois's
intimacy with the Americo-Liberian elite and their assumptions, Johnson
emphasized the profound cultural distinctions and power discrepancies
that existed between Americo-Liberians and native Liberians. Still, in so
doing, he also underscored native Liberian difference and limited their
agency by suggesting that European and U.S. intervention was on their
behalf. Native Liberians needed protection from the vicissitudes of the
emerging modern economy, Johnson concluded.[15]

Prominent Africans also entered the rhetorical fray. Eventual president of Nigeria Nnandi Azikiwe argued that the furor over the situation
in Liberia resulted from Western ethnocentrism: non-Africans could neither understand nor had the right to deplore African cultural practices
like pawning and polygamy.[16] Former Liberian president Edwin Barclay
resented the criticism and attention that Liberian labor practices received
and implied that the criticisms themselves were based on mistaken interpretations of the "racial ideal" that Liberia represented. Criticism of
Americo-Liberians was seen as tantamount to race disloyalty in much
of this rhetoric.[17]

Although these interpretations of the Liberian labor crisis differed in
many respects, they similarly created a discursive context in which Liberian labor lacked character and agency; indigenous Liberians were sub-
sumed into Africanist and anti-imperialist narratives. Although these

critiques of political economy and Western imperialism undoubtedly
contained a great deal of truth, their asymmetry and reliance on middle-
class conceptions of power and agency implied a black ethos rooted in the
assumptions of the middle class; that is, the political agency made possible
by these critiques all required a fairly European notion of civilization and
culture. In this rhetorical model, indigenous Liberia's distance from modernity implied that African Diasporic solidarity and identity required
a negation of contemporaneous Africa. By and large, these arguments
opted for paternal nostalgia for what Africa had once been or a projection
of what it could become.

"Slaves" Today

In 1930, funded by Euro-American publisher George Putnam, George
S. Schuyler traveled to Liberia to explore and expose the present condition of indigenous Liberian labor. Schuyler arrived in Monrovia in February 1931, interviewed President Edwin Barclay, and conducted a series
of tours of the Liberian hinterland. Aware that Liberian officials would
inhibit his investigation if they realized his agenda, Schuyler pretended
to be on vacation and secretly collected evidence of Liberian "slavery."[18]
Schuyler's ruse, his adoption of the "tourist" persona, allowed him un-
common access to the scenes of Liberian cultural and political life. Many
previous visitors, like W. E. B. Du Bois and representatives of Marcus
Garvey's Universal Negro Improvement Association, had spent most of
their time with the Americo-Liberian middle class and the indigenous
elite. Schuyler's dissimulation facilitated his movement through diverse
Liberian environments and his collection of clues, which he later used to
reveal the "truth" of the Liberian labor crisis.

Upon his return, Schuyler spent two months writing a novel that dra-
matized his experience in Liberia. In the novel's preface, he argued that,
like his journalism, his book was the product of his personal detective
work and his accumulation of evidence in Liberia. He wrote that the material for the narrative was gathered during a "three month sojourn on the
west coast of Africa in the early part of 1931," and that "All of the characters are taken from real life. Zo, Soki, Pameta, Big Georgie, and Chief
Bongomo answer to those names in Liberia today." He even claimed to
be "personally acquainted with them, as he is with most of the Americo-
Liberian characters who appear under fictitious names." However, despite

the novel's putative transparency and documentary nature, the preface also acknowledged its author's rhetorical intent. Of contemporary "slavery" as practiced throughout the globe, Schuyler wrote: "Regardless of the polite name that masks it while bloody profits are ground out for white and black masters, it differs only in slight degree from slavery in the classic sense, except that the chattel slaves lives were not held so cheaply. . . . If this novel can help arouse enlightened world opinion against this brutalizing of the native population in a Negro republic, perhaps the conscience of civilized people will stop similar atrocities in native lands ruled by proud white nations that boast of their superior culture." The novel as prefaced navigated curious rhetorical territory: it was a report of a foreign land and its social crisis, an argument for an attitude toward domestic and international politics, and an imaginative story. These diverse forms worked together to represent the "real" Africa, exemplified in the experiences of indigenous Liberians. Ultimately, however, as the preface and title suggest, the novel was also an attempt to document and illustrate the experience of contemporary "slaves."

Schuyler's sneakiness is partially explained by his profession. He was one of the most widely read African American journalists of the first half of the twentieth century, publishing in a variety of black American and Euro-American journals and newspapers. Though he wrote with a satirical bent over his entire career, he was indebted to the particular journalistic ethos of H. L. Mencken, whose acerbic commentaries exposed the perfidy of those he considered obfuscators and fascists. Mencken's style revealed truth through verbose and often hyperbolic characterizations of common sense. As editor of the (Baltimore) *American Mercury,* he published many of Schuyler's earliest and most prominent works, providing him with an audience beyond black newspapers and much needed income. Schuyler absorbed so much of his style and approach to writing from his mentor that he was often derisively referred to as the "Black Mencken." The genre of the sarcastic muckraker, so fundamental to early twentieth-century journalism, constituted an important dimension of the style of *Slaves Today.*[19]

Schuyler's novel portrays slavery through two apparently independent narratives. Michael Peplow identifies these narratives as the "Monrovia Thread," which exposes the corruption of the Americo-Liberian political elite, and the "Zo-Pametta Thread," in which a young indigenous Liberian couple struggle against gender-specific slaveries.[20] The Monrovia thread

details Tom Saunders's struggles against Americo-Liberian political bureaucracy and corruption. Specifically, Saunders and a few allies attempt
to achieve political power to wield against hypocritical clergymen and
incumbent politicians who are connected to corrupt business interests.
Saunders runs for president of Liberia and is defeated in a crooked election; consequently, slavery continues in Liberia in a new, more subtle
form. The Zo-Pametta thread begins in chapter two when the Americo-
Liberian District Commissioner interrupts the celebration of the marriage of the young hero Zo to his chief's daughter, Pametta. The District
Commissioner demands tribute from the tribe, and when he deems that
tribute inadequate, whips the tribe's chief and takes Pametta away to his
harem. Zo follows his bride into the jungle, is captured, and sent to Fernando Po to labor for the Spanish. Zo serves two years on the island, becomes enamored of Monrovia, the capital of Liberia, and then again seeks
out Pametta, who has been resisting her captor's overtures. Eventually,
Pametta is freed and Zo finds her diseased and dying, and he promises to
avenge her death. He kills the District Commissioner, is shot by a sentry,
and dies.

These two distinct narratives are united thematically, and together they
illustrate the ubiquity of "slavery": the slavery of politicians to bureaucracy,
the slavery of oppressed laborers, and the slavery of women bound in exploitative heterosexual relationships. The key to the novel is its assumption that slavery is the imposition of static social categories on individuals
and social relations that are fundamentally dynamic. Schuyler seems to
posit that politicians, workers, and women the world over endure stagnant
and immobilizing ways of thinking and calcified cultural spaces. Schuyler,
however, creates a special place for the uniquely Afro-Diasporic experience
within "slavery" as he defines it. That is, the basic understanding of slavery
in the text is sharpened by the particular treatment of these relations within
indigenous Liberian cultural practices. The text constructs a framework
within which black Americans may experience empathy for the indigenous
Liberian laborer, because, despite the distance of their geographical location, indigenous Liberians and black Americans undergo a common form
of exploitation and suffering based on the intersection of class and race.
Schuyler develops this connection by employing a generic figure of pulp
fiction — the detective protagonist — who possesses a dynamic identity and
traverses various cultural spaces illustrating the evils of static boundaries
and relations, especially for the black laborer.

The novel begins in earnest with the story of Zo's wedding and the rituals that celebrate it retold in the sympathetic voice of a curious outsider.
The narrator describes the dancing, native celebrants with a mix of awe
and envy: "This orchestra made fascinating, blood thirsting music as it ex-
ecuted a preliminary march from one end of Takama to the other. Naked
little boys and girls followed it yelling and capering. When they returned
a great circle was made by the people with the orchestra opposite the chief.
There was now to be individual dancing. Rival experts would display remarkable exhibitions of intricate footwork and gymnastics.... Youngsters
not yet in their 'teens would leap practically nude into the ring, flashing
like animated ebony in the afternoon sun."[21] This description of the wedding party identifies and celebrates the cultural practices of the people of
Takama. It reveals the author's fascination with the aesthetic components
of the ritual — the beauty, the athleticism, and the eroticism of the foreign.
Moreover, it highlights the distance between the cultural background of
the narrator and that of the native Liberians. The beauty and difference
of the cavorting dancers compels the narrator.

The narrator maintains this exoticizing voice throughout the novel,
describing Liberian cultural practices and Americo-Liberian politics with
the same remove. However, unlike contemporaneous primitivist and Africanist discourse, the narrator of *Slaves Today* employs an objective voice
to explain the function these practices serve in indigenous Liberian communities and their effect on indigenous Liberians.[22] Take, for example, the
character of the witch doctor Tolo. Tolo is introduced as the narrator details the ceremonies involved in Zo and Pametta's wedding. He performs
a number of rituals to predict the success of the marriage, and the narrator
describes Tolo's specific procedures in meticulous, objective detail. Although obviously detached from the rituals themselves as the description
implies, the narrator explains the function that Tolo's predictions serve
for his community. Like practitioners of politics "the world over," Tolo
had found it wise "to surround all his findings with an aura of mystery and
uncertainty, the better to hold the respect and confidence of his clients."
Similarly, later in the text, the Americo-Liberian president is described as
worried because, "like all successful candidates for office, he was finding
it easier to promise than pay off" — a pressing issue given that he believed
"a ruling class ... must be supported in leisure by those whom it ruled."[23]

By describing the functions of particular cultural traditions in their
lived contexts, the text is consistent with contemporaneous trends in

anthropology, but it challenges popular discussions of how black America related to African culture and aesthetics. For example, Alain Locke's 1925 essay "Legacy of the Ancestral Arts" called for an African American idiom derived from interpretation of African motifs. Although he valued African aesthetic forms and reconfigured dominant primitivist assumptions, Locke still argued for a deliberately monadic conception of African American expression achieved by removing African art from its context and denying its native cultural function.[24] In contrast, Schuyler's ethnographic description identifies Liberian cultural practices and makes no attempt to de-Africanize them. In fact, at a public debate about Liberia inspired by his novel and sponsored by the Native African Union in Harlem, Schuyler argued, "there is little wrong with the native civilization . . . the sooner the missionaries learn to leave God out of their work and allow the natives to follow their customs of dress and ethics which are far more sensible than those practiced in this country, the better it will be for all concerned."[25] Schuyler's novel attempts to understand these practices by placing them in both their local cultural contexts and a global political frame. Indeed, the text is full of similar moments that diagnose how dominant cultural practices of the elite hold onto power and impose an artificial stagnation on the dynamic potentiality of the underclass. This theme is evident in much of Schuyler's work.[26] For him, the ecstasies of religious experience and the structure of myth and ritual created community and maintained systems of power through their strategic clarity and gate-keeping vocabulary.

This critique of power may appear to be universal; perhaps the text is suggesting that bourgeois power perpetuates itself through the creation of static class distinctions irrespective of locality. Many of Schuyler's critics accused him of underemphasizing the significance of racial prejudice in the exploitation of Liberian labor.[27] Nevertheless, Schuyler's work suggests that, although the form of class-based oppression transcends political borders, its expression is culturally specific. Indeed, as is demonstrated in the novel's characterization of Liberian space, the African Diaspora has a particular experience with bourgeois power.

Slaves Today represents Liberian geography most frequently through comments about the country's oppressive heat or generic jungle foliage, which are used to create a fundamental binary between rural and urban spaces. Like the novel's description of Liberian cultural practices, the dissociation between the rural and the urban both exoticizes Liberian space *and* implies points of commonality with black America, suggesting that black Americans and indigenous Liberians share a position within modernity. Of Monrovia, Schuyler writes: "the one place where a man mightier than the District Commissioner sits and gives orders; an enormous place where thousands and thousands of people live without the onerous restrictions imposed by tribal laws and customs, a place where there are plenty of shillings to be made by everybody and anybody. Great iron canoes that could hold everybody in a big native town, come puffing into the harbor from across the waters — from distant, strange lands where the people's skins are white. A wonderful place Monrovia!"[28]

In this passage, Schuyler describes Monrovia with a mixture of awe and practical ambition; it is a space of magic and a place where industrious Liberians freed from the miasma of Americo-Liberian oppression and residual tradition and tribal authority can improve themselves. This description of Liberian geography echoes black America's particular experience with the dynamic of rural and urban space. Indeed, Schuyler's description of Monrovia brings to mind an African "City of Refuge," Rudolph Fisher's fictional account of Harlem published in Alain Locke's *The New Negro*. Fisher describes his protagonist's first experience with Harlem as initially one of wonder and disorientation: King Solomon Gillis was, "confronted suddenly by daylight . . . he felt as if he had been caught up in the jaws of a steam shovel, jammed together with other helpless lumps of dirt." Still, Gillis's shock at his dehumanization in the modern context eventually signifies opportunity. Later, the he realizes that "in Harlem, black was white. You had rights that could not be denied you; you had privileges, protected by law. And you had money. Everybody in Harlem had money. It was a land of plenty."[29]

Although each appreciation of the urban is typically modern, these descriptions of Monrovia and Harlem, respectively, evoke an experience with modernity particular to raced populations. Fundamentally, each assumes that issues of identity are responsible for the repressive force of the tradition — disempowerment was a function of who you were not what you had or did. Moreover, each expresses an ambivalent constellation of hope, wonder, and trepidation toward the modern. As Henry Louis Gates Jr. argues, European literary modernism grew from a European fear of standardization, from unease with the subordination of the individual to the dehumanizing forces of industrialization and modern warfare. In the African Diaspora, in contrast, standardization held promise of economic opportunity and assimilation into European democracies. Thus, the African Diaspora shared a particular hopefulness relative to urban space. Moreover, as Houston Baker argues, European literary modernism was preoccupied with the modern threat to white entitlement. The modern signified radical change, and this change assaulted tradition and the disposition of power in the status quo. According to these scholars, the disempowered within the African Diaspora had a particularly sanguine investment in the possibilities of modernity.[30]

The novel's characterization of Liberia creates a discursive space for black empathy with Africa's indigenous cultures and an opportunity for Pan-African community. The novel is faithful to the cultural particularity of indigenous Liberia, but it indexes these Liberian cultural practices to the operation of power against those disempowered because of their identity; its description of Liberia situates black people in diaspora and indigenous Liberia within the same position relative to modernity. In this sense, the novel argues that proximity to modernity does not exclude intimacy with the cultural dynamics of indigenous African modernity; indeed, the particularities of indigenous Liberian experience are a bridge to acknowledging Afro-disproic community. Both black America and indigenous Liberia are subject to the operation of power aimed at maintaining static social hierarchies and both also incubate the dynamism and ingenuity suggested by the characterization of Monrovia. Within the novel, this shared condition is given clear expression in the main character, Zo, a hero empowered to navigate diverse cultural and geographic spaces.

The Pulp Fiction Hero

Although Schuyler's novel includes a number of prominent characters, the story of Zo is the primary narrative; his wedding initiates the plot and the novel climaxes with his self-sacrifice in murdering the District Commissioner. Although a literary work, the novel employs the conventions of pulp fiction. Zo's nemesis, the obese, cigar-chomping, whiskey-swilling District Commissioner, evokes images of colonial self-indulgence popular in dime novels and contemporary popular cinema.[31] Zo himself also resembles a pop culture character type, the pulp fiction hero. In Zo, then, the novel employs the convention of the pulp fiction to articulate an Afro-Diasporic hero empowered by the resources of modernity.

The modern hero of popular fiction developed from the conventions of nineteenth-century serialized fiction. From 1842 to 1843 Eugène Sue published *Les Mystères de Paris,* the fictional exploits of an incredible hero in the face of pure villainy serialized in ten inserts in the newspaper *Le Journal des Debats.*[32] Although focused on Parisian street life, the stories vividly detailed sex and violence among the rich and the poor, pausing occasionally for moralizing commentaries and pleas for social reform. These digressions often emanated from the perspective of Rudolphe, the series' protagonist, whose moral vision and hyperbolic heroic agency derived from his position between the seedy underworld of the working class and the rarefied strata of the aristocracy.[33] Within a year of the translation and publication of Sue's stories in English, U.S. publishers published thirteen derivative novels, each using Sue's formula and set in a domestic context. The major deviation from Sue's formula, according to Ronald and Mary Saracino Zboray, was that U.S. narratives focused on the valorous exploits of the commoner. In a United States context, the French formulaic hero adopted the characteristics of the working class, and the hero's ability to move among multiple contexts became representative of the versatility of the "common" man.[34]

Near the turn of the century, a "post-frontier aesthetic" emerged in U.S. popular fiction; dime novels reacted against late nineteenth-century sentimentalist literature and the gendered female political idealism that was correlated with it, and ushered in a new period of "virilist realism" wherein limited resources mandated a Darwinist approach to accumulation. Accordingly, much popular fiction of this period celebrated masculinity, violence, and racial purity. In the early years of the twentieth century, this "red-blooded" fiction became localized in particular territories, giving birth to genres in various media such as Oriental and African adventure stories and films set on the "new frontiers of imperialism."[35] The heroes of these stories were defined by their liminal existence — their fluency both with the foreign territory in which they resided and with the echoes of their home that sounded in their behavior. They demonstrated an independent moral compass and existed in the righteous space between the powerful and the disempowered. Edgar Rice Burrough's much studied and profoundly racist Tarzan, who was of noble European birth but grew up among African apes, exemplifies this middle space.[36] Ironically, this motif was indebted to its proximity to the cultural traditions and raced populations it negatively characterized. As Ishmael Reed would eventually illustrate, the pulp fiction hero had much in common with the "trickster" of African American folklore.[37]

In the early years of the twentieth century this tendency in popular fiction returned to urban spaces, and the modern detective was born. The detective was a character who, like earlier heroes of French serialized fiction and of the U.S. frontier, exhibited a moral independence derived from his existence in the space between law and crime. The appeal of these novels lay in their ability to represent the putatively real form of the foreign in familiar terms. As Richard Slotkin argues, the "'hook' which drew readers into the seedy world of the detective was its promise to acquaint them with a world that was both exotic and hidden and undeniably real."[38] Thus the detective, as a translator of the distant, is a mediator of difference, an icon of both the foreign and the familiar.

Much of Schuyler's fiction employs a detective-like character as its protagonist. The hero of his first novel, *Black No More,* was a man named Max Disher, who was likely patterned on Rudolph Fisher, author of the African American detective novel *The Conjure Man Dies.* Though not an actual detective, Disher exemplified the character type: he was resourceful and able to negotiate multiple social spaces and categories — urban and rural, north and south, and, ultimately, black and white. Moreover, he spoke the languages of many classes, both the parlance of the street and the argot of privilege.[39] Schuyler's articulation of the pulp fiction hero is peculiar because he situates him in both U.S. cities and African jungles.[40] In *Slaves Today,* Zo is a Pan-African pulp fiction hero who provides a bridge between black America and indigenous Africa.

Despite the debilitating violence that he suffers at the hands of his Americo-Liberian oppressors, Zo is constantly in motion, looking and working for change, for return to Liberia or to liberate Pametta. On the boat headed to Fernando Po, Zo, "along with two or three of the bolder spirits," tried to kick down the door of the cabin in which they were held. When he first arrived on the island, unlike many of his fellow "slaves," Zo worked to escape. No passive victim of cruel circumstance, Zo is energized by the suffering he endures and, seasoned enough not to foment overt rebellion, he furtively collects information about possible escape. He asks a Bassa man named Georgie about stealing a boat, enquires about running away to the mountains. Zo studies his overseer and gradually learns English. Every time Zo's overseer spoke, Zo listened, and eventually, "he would repeat familiar words over and over to himself at night and during his work, until they were memorized." Zo performed his duties so well that he "seemed so tractable that no one thought of him planning to run away."[41] As characterized by Schuyler, Zo is no victim of slavery, nor is he a traditional picaro, buffeted by forces he cannot understand in a world beyond his control. Rather, he is an opportunist, a hero who can understand contexts, switch codes, and pursue his self-interest and independent moral vision.

Zo's heroic stature emanates from this mobility, his ability to function comfortably within cultural spaces in binary opposition: village and city, tribal authority and the power of the Americo-Liberian plutocracy. Defined by this mobility, Zo is not exclusively American or Gola, his tribal identification. Rather, he personifies a space between the two. He alone among his compatriots indentured on Fernando Po saves his meager income in hope of the life he will lead after he is freed from the island; his fellow tribe members fear the District Commissioner, while he repeatedly challenges him; and he is true to a monogamous relationship while the Liberians and Americo-Liberians around him are polygamous. Still, he also negotiates the jungle with aplomb, honors the traditions and customs of his tribe, and fears and respects the wisdom of Tolo the witchdoctor. Zo is not merely an American character transported to the jungle, mapping and navigating an African frontier. *Slaves Today* is more than the imposition of a U.S. value system on the exotic terrain of Africa or a casual homology designed to reach Schuyler's black American audience.[42] Rather, Zo is neither African nor American, but an agent empowered to be both. In this sense, like the pulp fiction hero and detective, Zo's agency has temporal and spatial dimensions. He is defined by his capacity for movement and versatility in the present, not by the static formulations of power or inherited racial and national identities. Zo embodied a renewed vitality shared by Africans and African Americans within modernity.

In the character of Zo, *Slaves Today* articulates a heroic, hybrid scion to respond to the modern challenges facing the African Diaspora. This character develops W. E. B. Du Bois's interpretation of black identity in modernity, translating the blessing of "prophetic sight" bestowed on those who suffer "double-consciousness" into a capacity for movement that characterizes the invigorated political agent.[43] In *The Souls of Black Folk,* Du Bois explained that the experience of race created a twoness in black Americans, an awareness of being both African and American. This awareness was manifest in a disembodied double vision wherein black Americans viewed their experience through both African American and Euro-American lenses. Later, in 1920's "The Souls of White Folk," Du Bois developed this concept to argue that this double vision also allowed privileged insight back into "whiteness" and the nature of race in modernity.[44] For Du Bois, black hybridity facilitated vision, awareness, insight, and cultural critique, not political or economic power; Schuyler's Pan-African fiction provided an alternative configuration of "twoness" that built upon and politicized Du Bois's vision. In Schuyler's novel, hybridity engendered political and economic agency that confronted logics of white supremacy and realized the potential of mass Pan-African culture.

Politics of Race, Diaspora, and Class

That racist images of black inferiority permeated U.S. culture in the 1930s is self-evident. Even progressive anthropology and sociology emerged in concert with alternative theories of human development that served more regressive agendas.[45] The exoticization of Africa in rhetoric that rationalized U.S. imperialist foreign policy further devalued black American experience; in particular, racist representations of black people were often coextensive with racist evaluations of Africa.

The Liberian labor crisis focused racist rhetoric on the prominent African republic. Liberia was considered a "failure" or an "embarrassment," an experiment in cultivating black republicanism gone awry.[46] This discourse often made comparisons between the apparent inability of the African nation to maintain a stable government or achieve economic viability with black struggles in the United States. Charles S. Johnson, noted black sociologist and member of the committee that investigated the Liberian situation, related in his diary that his colleague Dr. Cuthbert Christy made such arguments explicitly. According to Johnson, Christy thought that Africans were "standing still and 100 years behind England and France" and that "U.S. Negroes were 100 years behind whites."[47] Christy's equation of African and black American development argued for a paternalistic approach to black American and African political progress and against black involvement in the administration of Liberia's unrest. In Christy's racist calculus, the crisis resulted from an inherent lack of black political skill; therefore, it could not be solved by the assistance of African Americans whom he considered similarly retarded.

In some racist U.S. discourse, black American sympathy for the African republic was cited as further proof of their poor political acumen. Roosevelt's emissary to Liberia, Harry Mc Bride, criticized black American minister to Liberia Solomon Porter Hood for mistakenly importing race consciousness into a Liberian context: "Hood could have gotten filled up with race hatred while he was back in the US. . . . It took him nearly a year to forget he was black the time he first came out."[48] Although this statement suggests a distinct "Americanness" in black American identity, it also accuses Hood of political awkwardness. To Mc Bride, Liberia was a space in which black people had mistakenly aired their domestic political frustration. The inherent inability of black people to govern, to be self-sustaining, was clear from the country's lack of stability and from the awkward and misguided orientation to global citizenship implied by sympathy for Liberian laborers. Racist interpretations of the Liberian labor crisis buttressed the logic of white supremacy by undermining black identity in terms of political skill.

In contrast, the vision of black identity that emerged from Schuyler's anticolonial fiction confronted racist negation of black political agency. *Slaves Today* portrayed black agency through a vision of diaspora characterized by hybridity and dynamism and energized by the potential of labor in modernity. By expanding the parameters of black identity to include both the cultural particularities of the African Diaspora and the resources of mass culture, Schuyler's vision complicated black American political ethos and suggested that class-conscious black Americans were competent political actors in multiple contexts. Intimacy with "Africa" was no longer a political liability. Indeed, Afro-Diasporic political authority was derived from flexibility, from the impossibility of locating black interests within the boundaries of one state.

Slaves Today also expressed an innovative conceptualization of black mass culture. In the late nineteenth century, Booker T. Washington argued that restraint was the key to individual and collective progress.[49] In Washington's vision, black people around the globe needed to constrain their desire, political ambitions, and actual movement in order to achieve change. Schuyler, however, expressed a similar radical individualism, but one that privileged flexibility and travel. For Schuyler, the political voice was not sustained by "bucket" dropping, but by having multiple buckets, knowing when to drop them, and when to pick them back up and move on.

Moreover, *Slaves Today*'s articulation of mass Afro-Diasporic culture confronted powerful left-leaning rhetorics that sought to denationalize the struggle against colonialism by subsuming "race" in a larger narrative. However proletarian, Schuyler's vision was passionately anticommunist. While the ideas of the CPUSA enjoyed moderate success in black communities in the middle years of the 1930s, black America was never smitten by the party itself. In the early 1930s fewer than two hundred black Americans identified themselves as members of the Communist Party, while its national membership was over seventy-five hundred.[50] These numbers likely reflect a hesitancy on the part of some black Americans voluntarily to associate with yet another group subject to discrimination, but they also testify to ambivalence toward Euro-American style populism, naïve globalism, and the state of Russia. Many black Americans agreed with George Padmore's fundamental distrust of the party and its motivations.[51] Despite a youthful flirtation with socialism, Schuyler despised the party and spent most of his career exposing what he considered its primary evil: the war it waged against the individual. In his autobiography, *Black and Conservative,* Schuyler wrote, "what seems to have escaped the generality of writers and commentators is that [communism, fascism, and Nazism] are identical in having regimented life from top to bottom, in having ruthlessly suppressed freedom of speech, assembly, press and thought, and in being controlled by politicians . . . what is new about all these forms of government is that they are all controlled by politicians with a reformer complex; ex-revolutionaries who have gained power and have nobody to curb their excesses."[52]

The rigidity and hierarchal structure of the Communist Party that Schuyler recognizes were off-putting to many Euro- and black Americans. Schuyler's novel suggested that, like fascism (and one might conjecture, racism), communism over-simplified identity and stifled the creative agency inherent in mass culture. From this perspective, the Communist Party's internationalism did not provide a model for black political agency that respected the particularity of black American experience or that of the African Diaspora; it reduced models of black nationality to derivatives of a Russian ideal proletariat. The popular vision of the African Diaspora presented in *Slaves Today,* however, represented a black American political voice that negated narratives focused on either race or class. Schuyler's more dynamic relationship with contemporary Africa suggested a complex black American identity and an invigorated black political agency that denied reductionist appreciations of black American and proletarian identity.

Furthermore, *Slaves Today* was published during the time of a radical change in media and popular culture Michael Denning has called the "Laboring of American culture."[53] Denning argues that at the end of the 1930s a new sense of "labored" United States culture emerged. He documents this change as evident in the appearance of the term "labor" in popular discourse, the proletarianization of cultural production in which workers became artists, cultural production as an industry, the social democratic culture of the New Deal, and increased representations of the working class in works of art. This novel demonstrates the working of this process in black public discourse relative to political crises around the globe. Denning suggests that the laboring of U.S. culture was intricately linked with global antifascism, but this chapter illustrates how the laboring of black American culture had specifically diasporic dimensions; *Slaves Today* demonstrates how the conventions of popular fiction figured in an African American public sphere. The character of the mass or popular hero took on diasporic dimensions in response to this specific geopolitical crisis. In this novel, the detective or hipster, empowered by his hybridity, became a metaphor for international citizenship and political empowerment in a global arena. In addition, as black American public discourse became more reflective of and responsive to the interests of labor, it also became more engaged in the dynamics of African culture and experience; thus the conventions of the pulp fiction novel produced a more proletarian conceptualization of Pan-African identity.

Black America and Africa

The Liberian crisis itself, like the occupation of Haiti, opened the way for black American involvement in diplomatic posts. Charles S. Johnson was one of many black Americans to travel to Liberia in a governmental capacity. While serving in these posts black Americans represented an "American" government and a Euro-American president, but they also created political and economic relationships with African elites. Moreover, black American foreign service was reported upon widely in the black press, lending added prominence to African issues, increasing the black American audience for news about Africa, and articulating a space for subsequent public arguments about Africa and its diaspora. For example, Melvin

Tolson's "Libretto for the Republic of Liberia" was written as a response to a close reading of *Slaves Today*.[54] Texts like *Slaves Today* and the "Libretto for the Republic of Liberia" spoke to a developing curiosity about Africa and a desire to understand Africa not as a tourist but as a member of a similar class.

In addition, this crisis and the empowered political voice that arose from it, was one factor that altered the course of domestic policy by putting black American interests in the forefront of the 1928, 1932, and 1936 national elections. During this period, despite pressing issues with the domestic economy, foreign policy loomed large, and black America shifted its allegiance to the Democratic Party. In fact, President Hoover shaped his policy regarding the Liberian labor crisis in order to win black votes.[55]

In his review of *Slaves Today*, published in *The Crisis*, W. E. B. Du Bois wrote of Schuyler, "in all of his writings, save this, he stood on the solid ground of his personal knowledge. He knew America," but in this latest book on Liberia, Schuyler had "missed his background." He did not realize the "history of Liberia and of present-day imperialism and industry in Africa."[56] According to Du Bois, Schuyler's novel, by foregrounding the story of a particular "slave," missed a more honorable history and the more complicated present. By telling the story of a contemporary native Liberian, Schuyler had omitted Liberia's glorious past, the history of "the men who have made Liberia, Roberts, Russwurm, Johnson, Barclay, and others, [who] are as fine a set of gifted and devoted human beings as ever worked the problem of human uplift."[57] This review demonstrates how Du Bois continued to consider Pan-African unity as derived from a debt to a shared past. Schuyler's novel saw diasporic unity in the shared economic and cultural conditions of the present. Although far from a realist tableau of Africa or an insightful critique of political economy, *Slaves Today* articulated a shift toward exploring the interconnections between the concerns of indigenous African populations and black American workers without relying exclusively on the language of class.

As the 1930s progressed, Schuyler revisited Africa frequently in his short fiction and essays. From 1933 to 1936 he published a series of five novellas in the *Pittsburgh Courier* that dealt with African themes and locales. Some of these stories abandoned any anthropological pretense for imaginative visions of what Africa could be. "Black Empire," for example, was a science fiction account of what Africa might be like if run by a black American scientist. Other stories grew from current events in world politics. "An Ethiopian Murder Mystery" was a response to the Italian invasion of Ethiopia. It was serialized in conjunction with historical essays and foreign correspondence from Ethiopia by Schuyler's friend Joel Augusts Rogers. Together, these texts about Ethiopia produced an upswing in the circulation of the *Pittsburgh Courier* never seen in black American newspapers up to then; in the late 1930s, black America understood the African Diaspora through Ethiopia, and black American anticolonialists spoke in its defense.

CHAPTER 5

Ethiopia Is Now

J. A. Rogers and the Italian Invasion of Ethiopia

WHEN HE RESPONDED to the Liberian labor crisis, George Schuyler expressed a black ethos that encompassed the African Diaspora and echoed with the voice of labor. His novel *Slaves Today* suggested that black workers around the globe shared a position within modernity: they were subject to the dehumanizing bureaucracies of the bourgeoisie and the imposition of racial thinking upon their daily lives, both of which created discrete, calcified cultural spaces. The main character of the novel exhibited an ability to navigate these artificially distinct contexts, and this "mobility" served as the ground for black American empathy with Africa. In this sense, the novel told of an African Diaspora empowered to resist colonial institutions and states of mind, whether those colonial institutions existed in Africa or the United States.

The rhetoric of black American anticolonialism continued to develop throughout the 1930s. At the close of the decade, people of African descent turned to Ethiopia and their public argument interpreted the African Diaspora as a coherent political concept, one that admitted ontological difference but did not subordinate African culture to a Western ideal.

Ethiopia has long figured in religious and nationalist discourse in the African Diaspora. What "Ethiopia" meant often reflected political developments there. For example, after the country repelled the Italian invasion at Adowa in 1896, black churches in both the United States and South Africa assumed names like Abyssinian, Ethiopian, or Kushite (a biblical tribe associated with modern-day Ethiopia).[1] Through affiliation with Ethiopia, each congregation interpolated its parishioners into a fundamentally Christian agency that transcended state and geographic boundaries. At the turn of the century "Ethiopian" suggested a synecdochical relationship between a member of a displaced elect community and its spiritual and geographic center.[2]

Marcus Garvey's quasi-ecclesiastical rhetoric suffused this tradition with the political activism of contemporaneous Pan-Africanisms. For Garvey, "Ethiopia" was the omphalos of a distinctly black symbolic universe, a spiritual center to orient black people in their contest with European nationalisms. As Garvey receded from prominence in the late 1920s, his interpretation of Ethiopia as both a spiritual and literal goal for black people in diaspora retained some currency. In 1927 Rabbi Arnold Ford explored the possibility of immigration to Ethiopia. Years later, he and his protégé, Rabbi Mathew, led a group of sixty-six from a Harlem synagogue to settlement in Ethiopia.[3] This expedition was an early, large-scale attempt by people of African descent to make the ideal of Ethiopia a political reality. Even though the colony in 1934 failed to achieve a black American Jerusalem in Africa, the community's founding spoke to Ethiopia's powerful symbolism in the black imaginary and to a particular confluence of spiritual ideas and political rhetoric that operated in the Great Depression's matrix of race and economy. Rabbi Mathew's expedition, not unlike Father Divine's Peace Mission, confronted white supremacy and the insolvencies of the Depression with the liberatory potential of an alternate context. New spaces, in Ethiopia or in Divine's "Heaven" communes, provided a transcendent environment in which black people could transform themselves. Indeed, within Divine's communes, converts left their gender behind, practiced total celibacy, never uttered the word "race," and took new names.[4] Likewise, the dream of emigration to a holy "Ethiopia" encouraged black Americans to perceive themselves with fresh eyes, as pilgrims, as members of an elect community operating in a metaphysical terrain above the compromised space of political behavior.

In 1935 Italy invaded Ethiopia, and people of African descent turned to public argument to interpret their relationship with the last free state in Africa and its symbolic configurations in their discursive past. In speeches, protests, pamphlets, and newspapers, activists argued for economic, political, and military action on behalf of Ethiopian sovereignty.[5] This rhetoric did not cohere into a consensus about "black" foreign policy regarding the invasion. Indeed, by and large, black Americans interpreted the invasion as more than a foreign policy issue. For many, the invasion of Ethiopia had decidedly local dimensions. It was immediate, an act in the international contest between black and white, colonizer and colonized, that raged simultaneously in Ethiopia and Harlem. As Roi Ottley recalled in his 1943 memoir of Harlem and black culture, *New World a-Coming: Inside Black America,* the Italian invasion of Ethiopia "permeated every phase of Negro life."[6] In the 1960s, looking through a broader historical lens, John Hope Franklin viewed the Italian invasion of Ethiopia as the most important moment of international conflict for African American identity in the twentieth century. He observed: "Almost overnight even the most provincial among Negro Americans became international-minded."[7]

Scholars in diverse fields have documented black America's response to the invasion, but the rhetorical dimensions of the crisis remain unstudied.[8] Specifically, scholars have yet to explore how rhetorical expression shaped perception of the Italian invasion as a crisis for black America and to investigate how this rhetorical solidarity with Ethiopia influenced black political culture. To better understand these issues and black collective identity at the close of the 1930s, I shall analyze Joel A. Rogers's pamphlet "The Real Facts about Ethiopia." Rogers was one of the most prolific and influential commentators on Africa and black history at the time.[9] This pamphlet combined political, historical, anthropological, and religious research into a single argument for black American solidarity with Ethiopia. The pamphlet's popularity and comprehensiveness make it an apt point of entry into the rhetorical texture of black America's response to the Italian invasion of Ethiopia.

In this chapter I first argue that the Italian invasion of Ethiopia precipitated a rhetorical crisis in which black America's relationship to Ethiopia became contested. Second, I contend that Rogers's pamphlet resolves this crisis by critiquing the nature of race under colonialism and illustrating how state boundaries and racial categories are coordinate, strategic operations of colonial power. Third, I demonstrate how the text creates an alternative racial context — a secular myth of Ethiopia — that does not rely on a colonial definition of race. "Ethiopia" is reinvented as a figure of racially heterogeneous community, a community bound together through shared experience in political and mythical time. This temporal frame recollects the dispersed elements of the African Diaspora, providing a framework for understanding transnational black community. At the close of the 1930s, this anticolonial perspective influenced the tenor and focus of black political culture in the United States.

The collective identity embodied by this text was founded in the African Diaspora, but it was distinct from nineteenth-century appreciations of Ethiopia as the font of diasporic salvation and from twentieth-century Garveyite mythology. Specifically, it departed from the diffusionist paradigm of discrete, pure cultural spaces related in hierarchy and instead suggested a sense of Afro-Diasporic collective identity characterized by hybridity, equity, and consubstantiality.

The Italian Invasion of Ethiopia

After the European colonial dash for Africa that closed the nineteenth century, Liberia and Ethiopia remained the only "independent" nations in Africa. Liberia was technically independent, but it suffered an economic occupation. Largely beholden to U.S. and European corporations, burdened by foreign loans, and watched closely by the League of Nations because of its past human rights abuses, Liberia could not resist European colonial encroachment either within its own borders or in Africa more broadly. Ethiopia, however, had maintained an independent monarchy that traced its patrimony back to the Bible, its royal court enjoyed intimacy with European monarchies, and the nation as a whole appeared poised to reap the fruits of modernity on its own terms.[10]

In 1935 the Italian government prepared to invade Ethiopia, invoking the glorious legacy of imperial Rome and citing a skirmish between Ethiopian troops and Italian soldiers on Ethiopian soil. As tensions between Ethiopia and Italy heightened, European powers were either silent or openly supportive of Italian aggression. Despite the provision against international aggression established in the Kellog-Briand Pact of 1928, the League of Nations refused to censure Italy's violation of Ethiopia's sovereignty.[11] Ignoring an agreement not to sell arms to either combatant and to impose sanctions, League members continued to sell Italy the oil it required to fuel its mechanized troops. In practice, Europe's principle of neutrality crippled Ethiopian self-defense but did not significantly hamper Italy's ability to make war.[12]

The Italian government that violated Ethiopia's borders in 1935 had intimate ties to U.S. capital. Wealthy American Zionists supported Mussolini's rise to power and donated to his government in the hope of obtaining Italian support for a Jewish state. Henry Ford and other wealthy U.S. industrialists supplied economic aid to Mussolini and were responsible for sympathetic portrayals of the Italian dictator in domestic periodicals. Popular American icons like Will Rogers publicly supported Italian fascism, and mainstream periodicals with ties to the J. P. Morgan Company like *The New Republic* and *The Saturday Evening Post* editorialized in favor of Mussolini.[13]

Western complicity in Mussolini's colonial ambitions and the interests of U.S. capital in the Italian fascist regime encouraged black people to identify with Ethiopia; the political climate of the invasion suggested analogous relationships between international and domestic phenomena: Mussolini's avarice recalled the graft and decadence of U.S. industrialists, Ethiopian suffering echoed black America's struggle for political and economic progress, and the League of Nation's hypocrisy and impotence resonated with the U.S. government's inability and unwillingness to protect the lives and rights of African Americans. Many black Americans viewed the United States' official statement of neutrality in 1935 as a tacit endorsement of Mussolini's regime motivated by racial prejudice. People like Joseph Johnson were left with the impression that the "U.S. will not help Ethiopia because she is black. She won't do no more for Ethiopia than she will do to stop mob rule in the south."[14] Thus, the Italian invasion of Ethiopia complicated black America's relationship to the African Diaspora and U.S. democracy.

"Of What Race Are the Ethiopians?"

In its political context, the meaning of the Italian invasion to black America pivoted on a discursive negotiation of the racial status of the Ethiopian people. This general controversy had two related dimensions: were Ethiopians "black" enough for political solidarity with black Americans, and how would racial affinity between Ethiopians and African Americans matter in the context of white supremacy?

Despite Ethiopia's traditional significance for black Americans, sympathetic and accurate information about the contemporary nation and its relationship to the African Diaspora was scarce. At the close of 1934, Carter G. Woodson wrote a letter to the editor of *Afro-American Magazine* in which he lamented, "With the approach of Negro history week, many teachers are planning to build their programs around Ethiopia, but historians can give them little assistance. . . . [T]he books which are already available supply little of much needed information and most of those now tumbling in large numbers from the presses are not intended to inform the people but to exploit the gullible American public, which feasts upon falsehoods and scandal."[15] Indeed, white European and European American tourists published travelogues that detailed their experiences in Ethiopia, relied on racist evaluations of the continent as a whole, and adopted the format of the adventure novel. William Chaplin Watts's *Blood and Ink* and Mortimer Durand's *Crazy Campaign: A Personal Narrative of the Italo-Abyssinian War,* for example, characterized Ethiopia as comically barbaric and a playground for the bold.[16] Responding to black American appetites for more accurate information about Ethiopia, *The Afro-American Magazine* suggested that its readers attend to Gordon McCreagh's *The Last of Free Africa,* a collection of pro-Ethiopian articles that lauded the "Island of Christianity in a sea of black paganism."[17] McCreagh's credibility as a resource for African history, despite his jaundiced appreciation of the African continent as a whole, reveals the dearth of information about Ethiopia available to U.S. audiences in the middle 1930s. The texts that did address the race of the Ethiopians tended to place them in a racist category suffused with the derogatory assumptions of primitivism or to laud them through dissociation from the rest of Africa. Prominent Ethiopians contributed to the uncertainty surrounding Ethiopia's relationship to the African Diaspora. The government of Ethiopia considered its sovereignty evident, so it did not participate in the Pan-African conferences held in the early years of the twentieth century. In addition, Ethiopian nobility publicly denied any membership in the "Negro" race.[18] In 1897, Haitian poet Benito Sylvain asked Emperor Menelik, Haile Selassie's predecessor, for financial support to "uplift the race." According to U.S. diplomat Robert Skinner, Menelik's answer was negative; his response was "I am not a Negro . . . I am Caucasian." Still, at the close of World War I the Ethiopian government sent a delegation to congratulate the U.S. government and foster diplomatic relations between the two nations. In August 1919 members of the delegation attempted to dine at the National Democratic Club in New York City and were denied entry because they were "black." Significantly, this slight received a great deal of coverage in African-American newspapers.[19]

Euro-American scholars denied any affinity between black Americans and Ethiopians. For instance, in 1935 Euro-American intellectuals argued that black American sympathy for Ethiopia was a "hollow groundless form of idealism, based entirely on misconceptions."[20] Some averred that Ethiopian civilization was too advanced to be the product of a Negro race and posited ancient white ancestors for modern-day Ethiopians: "Maintaining that indigenous Africans lacked the capacity to create the complex state structures found among the Abyssinians, white commentators on African ethnography typically attributed a Caucasian rather than a Negro ethnicity to the Ethiopians. Whether racial liberals or conservatives, they generally referred to the sharp-featured Abyssinians as Hamites—a mythical dark branch of the white race that had allegedly introduced high civilization to parts of the African continent."[21] Other Euro-American journalists and popular anthropologists claimed that Ethiopians were not of "Negro stock" because of their reluctance to call themselves "negro," while others interpreted photos and their personal experience as proving that Ethiopians did not have Negro features and were therefore Arabian or Hamite in origin. In this sense, both Ethiopians and racist commentators on Ethiopian ethnicity maintained that Ethiopia's proximity to European modernity erased its cultural, historic, and even geographic relationship to Africa.

This discursive context is significant for three reasons. First, it highlights the authority of a specific rhetoric of blackness at this historical moment. The characteristics of authentic blackness were both physiological and anthropological in nature, but, interestingly, the barometer of African-ness in domestic racial politics was decidedly New World. Thus, Ethiopians from Africa could be less "African" than African Americans who might or might not have ever visited the continent. Second, arguments in favor of African Diasporic solidarity were rhetorically problematic. Such appeals were sometimes interpreted by white supremacists as a sign of gullibility or as a political miscalculation. Third, black America had a significant interest in and need for an independent field of knowledge, not just about American or even black American history, but also about black American experience in the context of the African Diaspora.

Speaking to this need, academic intellectuals like Carter G. Woodson and W. E. B. Du Bois created sympathetic knowledge about the African Diaspora.[22] Meanwhile, black popular intellectuals self-published pamphlets about Africa and African America that reached a mass black audience. Hubert Harrison's 1919 *When Africa Awakes* and George Wells Parker's 1918 *The Children of the Sun*, for example, countered white supremacy with visions of a redeemed Africa.[23] Pamphlets like these were inexpensive to publish and purchase and were read many times, being circulated through various parties, public spaces, restaurants, barbershops, and so on. Moreover, they often provided the content for orations by Harlem's many street speakers. As Myrtle Pollard argued in her 1937 dissertation at the City College of New York, "Harlem as Is," street speakers provided political and cultural leadership to black urban communities: "One person will be made to recall the years of segregation at the Alhambra theater on Seventh Avenue and 126th street; another will be reminded of having his money returned at Loew's Victoria on 125th street in preference to allowing him to sit in an empty orchestra."[24] Thus the street speaker in black urban centers accomplished more than just oral journalism or a recitation of current events; he stimulated public memory in the service of politics. Street speakers related local, national, and global political issues to the memory of everyday experiences. The rhetoric of a street speaker, for example, could equate the real, personal memory of a Jim Crow streetcar with ignominies suffered by black communities abroad: the unrepentant venality of Western colonialism in Africa could evoke an experience with an Italian American shopkeeper in Harlem or Chicago's South Side.

Shared in public urban spaces and cited by street speakers, pamphlets reached specific audiences without having to rely on mainstream editorial protocols, major advertisers, or industries of distribution. Those that did include advertising usually notified readers of other works by the text's author or suggested like reading from another popular intellectual on a similar topic. Pamphlets cited each other and the experiences of their authors and, in their oral delivery by street speakers, evoked the experiences of their audiences. In this sense, they facilitated the development of a field of independent, self-referential knowledge in black urban life.

Joel Augustus Rogers was one of the more popular pamphleteers.[25] He wrote pamphlets that were sympathetic to the African continent as a whole and were based on his personal experiences in Africa. In 1930 Rogers was appointed the first official foreign correspondent for a black newspaper and traveled to Ethiopia to cover the inauguration of Ras Tafari as Emperor Haile Selassie. In 1936 he returned to Ethiopia, this time as a war correspondent. Later that year, when he returned to the United States, he published a pamphlet titled *The Real Facts about Ethiopia*. This pamphlet was both a compilation of his research into Ethiopian history and an argument for black solidarity with the Ethiopian people.

The Real Facts about Ethiopia

Rogers's pamphlet is a collection of brief essays, timelines, personal reflections, and pictures. In subheadings, the text addresses topics such as "The Sex Lure of Ethiopia," "Slavery in Ethiopia," "What the Ethiopians Might Expect under Italian Rule," and a "General History of Ethiopia." The individual sections weave together the author's personal experience in Ethiopia and in the United States with journalistic insight and academic and biblical sources.

The first section of the text, "Of What Race Are the Ethiopians?" distinguishes between "American" and "universal" notions of "Negro." Through this distinction Rogers denaturalizes race within the boundaries of a state and proposes an alternative, more material sense of racial community in a global context. The text's critique of American race begins by asserting that the label "Negro" is applied with ludicrous imprecision in the United States. As illustration Rogers cites Hubert Harrison's encounter with the U.S. government during his naturalization proceedings. Harrison, though "coal black," was designated white because of his Danish surname. His experience proved that "Negro" was a capricious term applied inaccurately by a bureaucracy out of touch with reality. In this first, American context, "Negro" is so haphazardly applied that it is "sometimes caste, sometimes race, sometimes both." Moreover, in order to define who is truly "Negro" in the United States, "a scrambled brain is the first essential. And a touch of lunacy qualifies one as an expert."[26] Despite the sloppiness, this act of categorization managed to establish discrete cultural spaces, concrete and artificial borders between black and white. For example, Rogers states that the "American" sense of "Negro . . . includes all the shades from black to light yellow and white, and all textures of hair from silky blond to tightly curled wool."[27] This American sense of race imposed artificial categories on the self-evident complexity of human social groups and identities. Fundamentally, then, race in its American context was both artificial and irrational.

The political processes that created this artificial dichotomy between black and white in the United States also created subject and abject

classes. "Negro" in an American context was applied to "peoples of native African and Arabian descent" in "an attempt by the English-speaking
to denote social status." Thus, the creation of distinct racial types perpetuated the discrepancy in power between those positioned to create
the fiction of race and those who lived with race within a state's borders.
Popular portrayals of Emperor Haile Selassie provided further evidence
of this relationship between "race-ing" and status. Rogers indicted U.S.
newspapers for depicting Selassie as light-skinned, when in actuality he
was "lightish black-brown" and considerably "darker than one would infer
from the published pictures of him."[28] Thus, the text understands racial
classification as fundamentally a tool of power.

     In contrast, in its "universal" sense, race is self-evident and bridges the
boundaries of particular states. Rogers describes the universal sense of race
in order to demonstrate the depth and scope of the relationship between
race in America and colonialism and to supply the ground for his eventual
articulation of Afro-Diasporic racial solidarity in a secular myth of Ethiopia. In stark contrast to the "American" sense of the term, race in its universal sense is obvious to an untutored eye. Anyone who has experienced
it can recognize racial reality *and* the subterfuge of those who would establish and enforce artificial racial categories: "In reality, there are truly
only two varieties of mankind, the black and the white. All the others, the
Mongolian and the Indian, are in between. This is a commonsense view.
But in ethnology, as in phrenology and theology, there is a need for a mass
of mystifying names in order to impress the uninformed." The universal
sense of race is not tied to a particular institution nor to a specific space
or sense of borders — its stability is due to the repetition of *moments* of
recognition, observing the variegation, complexity, and shared interests
that suffuse human community. These authentic moments of racial solidarity exist in opposition to the creation of race by the state. Moreover,
the universal sense of race implies a continuum of racial identification;
although black and white are polar opposites, racial grades like Mongolian and Indian punctuate the space between the polarities. In its global,
universal sense, race occurs in grades — shades of black and white. This
racial continuum creates a sense of blackness that may include Africans in
America and in Africa: both communities exist toward the black half of
the racial spectrum.

     Equally important, however, the universal sense of race is not tied to a
particular institution. It is not grounded in a specific geographic space, nor

is it shaped by political borders or derived from an ethnic origin. Refuting the popular claim that Ethiopians were of Asiatic ancestry and thus not African, Rogers argues, "white people have been living in the New World only five centuries. Does one still call the descendants of Europeans in America, European?"[29] The answer for Rogers is an emphatic no, because racial community in its universal sense is produced through perception of commonality in the present rather than through a debt to history, a shared geographic space, or state authority. Racial solidarity is recognized, not certified; and experience with "reality" beyond the stultifying physical and ideological borders of "America" is the only qualification needed to perceive racial community in its true form.

Other influential black Americans interpreted the crisis in Ethiopia in a similar fashion — namely, as proof that the globe was polarized into an opposition between political solidarity that transcended state boundaries and racial community as defined by the state. W. E. B. Du Bois, for example, came to the same conclusion, using very similar reasoning, in an October 1935 article titled "The Inter-Racial Implications of the Italo-Ethiopian Crisis: A Negro View."[30] After acknowledging surface similarities between some people, citing "pictures of Abyssinians now widely current," he stated: "of course there are not and never were any 'pure' Negroes any more than there are any 'pure' whites or 'pure' yellows. Humanity is mixed to its bones."[31] Du Bois understood race as having a symbolic dimension.[32] Particular symbolic constructions of racial community served specific interests: "The belief that racial and color differences make exploitation of colonies necessary and justifiable was too tempting to withstand. As a matter of fact, the opposite was the truth; namely that the profit from exploitation was the main reason for the belief in race difference."[33] Du Bois argued that in the contest over colonies, European states created race. Race was an effect of state and economic power — racial community was created as a negative product of exploitation. He suggested that Ethiopia represented an alternative sense of community: Ethiopia was free from "race-ing" relationships.[34] Indeed, it was "an example and a promise of what a native people untouched by modern exploitation and race prejudice might do."[35]

In this text, published at a critical juncture in Du Bois's life and thought (and in black America's relationship to the African Diaspora), Du Bois implied that "race" had multiple valences: it could serve state power and create artificial distinctions between people, or it could be "natural" and reflect an authentic, complicated, international community. Like Rogers's pamphlet, Du Bois's article interpreted Italian imperialism as evidence of binaries imposed on the geopolitical scene. The entire globe was divided in terms of exploiter and exploited, artificial and authentic, and, ultimately, race-ing and raced.

As Mathew Pratt Guterl argues in his study *The Color of Race in America, 1900–1940,* in the late teens and early twenties, the concept of race in the United States underwent significant change. In prewar nationalisms race was defined by ethnicity and inherent, biological characteristics. In this milieu Irish, German, and white Anglo-Saxon were coordinate but distinct racial categories. As a result of political pressures, social change, and intellectual developments related to World War I, the myriad "ethnic" races that existed at the turn of the century gradually fused into fewer categories; race increasingly referred to color or to position within the global dynamics of imperialism, and "whiteness" and global "blackness" emerged.[36] This development can be seen in the rhetoric of Lothrop Stoddard, Madison Grant, and others who diagnosed the bifurcation of the globe with some anxiety.[37] In contrast, the critique offered by Rogers and Du Bois acknowledged the polarization of the globe and its attendant impending apocalypse but believed that neither was necessarily bad news.

African Americans throughout the United States interpreted the conflict in similar, stark, black-and-white terms. In a letter to the editor of the *Pittsburgh Courier,* physician Joe Thomas of Cleveland, Ohio, argued that "every son and daughter of African descent" should not "desert our Race in Africa. We must stand 'One for all, All for One.'"[38] Another letter to the editor of the *New York Tribune* opined: "Ethiopia is the land of our heritage. . . . This is a war of black against white."[39]

The "universal" sense of racial identification that emerges in these interpretations of the Italian invasion appears to replicate some of the very assumptions of the colonial, "American" paradigm it critiques. Rogers diagnoses the geopolitical scene as having two fundamentally opposed camps, white and black; these definitions pivot on a dichotomy between white and non-white, oppressor and non-oppressor. In this sense, it seems as though Rogers's universal sense of race does not really escape the context of colonialism; indeed, his universal sense of race depends upon colonialism through its opposition to colonial practices. At first blush, then, the "universal" sense of racial solidarity is, in Mark McPhail's terminology, "complicit" in the rhetoric of negative difference. In his analysis of the rhetoric of Afrocentricity, McPhail argues that potentially progressive rhetoric is complicit in the logic of racism if it posits inter-racial relations as a "conflict of essentially competitive world views."[40] Rogers's antagonism between American and universal racial politics, be-tween the forces of white imperialism and an international anticolonial community, appears to rely on just such a polarized opposition.

However, Rogers's anticolonial, "universal" citizenship grounded in "race" does retain some progressive potential. First, it inverts primitivist and white supremacist conceptions of Old and New World intellectual milieus. Since the Enlightenment, thinkers and rhetors interpreted the non-Western world as the irrational other of the centered, Western sub-ject.[41] Rogers's critique exposes the patina of rationality that cloaks the caprice and self-interest of U.S. racial politics, implying that it is in fact the rest of the world that has privileged access to reality. Indeed, his for-mulation of race argues that the "universal" experience of race is the norm from which the artificial, "American" sense deviates; in so doing, Rogers rhetorically constructs both blackness and whiteness from the perspective of one who has *experienced* race rather than from abstract principle.[42]

Second, this critique illustrates the complicity of bourgeois institu-tions in the perpetuation of racial inequity and thus interrogates the sys-tems and structures of racism. The argument identifies the relationship between bourgeois knowledge industries (like ethnology and the main-stream media), the state, and the categorization of people into subject and abject classes. Thus, the critique has power though its opposition, not only to colonialism, but to bourgeois sensibilities and institutions. As a critique of the systems of racism and Western imperialism, Rogers's rhetoric complicates the notion of "complicity." For, as Kirt Wilson ar-gues, complicit rhetoric becomes racist "only when it reinforces *systems* that produce racially disparate power relations."[43] Although it is complicit in some aspects of colonial discourse, then, Rogers's critique of global sys-tems of domination intervenes in structures that perpetuate racism.

Third, by casting U.S. racial politics as parochial, the text creates the opportunity for a more inclusive and expansive environment in which ra-cial subjects may take form, a space that is true to the complexity of raced experience. *The Real Facts about Ethiopia* gives texture to this alternative context through its commemoration of Ethiopia.

The Figure of Ethiopia

The text of Rogers's pamphlet combines anthropological, historical, and journalistic modes of writing in its description of Ethiopia. These empirical approaches are faithful to the particularity of Ethiopian culture and history. However, the text also employs Ethiopia as a metaphor for a new, international context in which black community can be performed, a space free from the artificial political borders and racial categories created by Western imperialism. The text characterizes Ethiopia as heterogeneous and borderless; it is dispersed and achieves coherence not because of the borders of its state or its consistent racial essence. Rather, Ethiopian community is defined as a shared experience in time.

Initially, the text establishes surface similarities between African Americans and ancient and modern Ethiopians. Still, the text undermines its own assertion of surface, physiological similarity through its inclusion of photos of Ethiopians that demonstrate a widely diverse field of physical characteristics. These pictures mediate the exoticism of the Ethiopian people by displaying the diversity of Ethiopian appearances. For example, the text includes several pictures of Emperor Selassie and Ethiopians of a variety of social classes and physical types. They portray members of different tribes, ostensibly displaying the "Negro" features of each. However, the individuals depicted possess such radically diverse physiognomies that their inclusion actually reinforces the text's argument against simple constructions of race that rely exclusively on appearance, biology, or the possibility of racial purity. The photos illustrate Ethiopian existence as variegated, and therefore as complicated and diverse as that of any other "normal" people. Through these images, the text addresses the exotic nature of the Ethiopian subject — Ethiopians are neither pure black Africans nor pure black African Americans. Instead, they are "normal," mixed. Thus, these photos support the text's argument that Ethiopia is without the "purity" that characterizes race as it is treated within the political borders created by Western colonialism. Indeed, according to Rogers's history, culturally and politically, Ethiopians have never policed racial categories, they "have never drawn a color line."[44]

This portion of the text provides a key to its fundamental epistemological assumptions. The pictures appear to reinforce the adage that seeing is believing; they provide empirical evidence of the Ethiopian racial "type." However, they illustrate no consistent physiognomy — thus the pictorial evidence appears to rebut the text's fundamental argument for Afro-American and Ethiopian identification by undercutting the possibility of an identifiable Ethiopian character. Still, these pictures function enthymetically, and through a materially specific hermeneutic protocol, a shared "common sense," the empirical realities they represent reaffirm the impossibility of a concrete understanding of race. In other words, ironically, the pictures identify what "everyone" knows is unidentifiable.

Rogers makes a similar argument about the complexity and dynamism of Ethiopia's social classes. Curiously, Ethiopia's practice of slavery provides his main evidence. He argues that slavery in Ethiopia is not a function of racial (or any other) identity. Indeed, it encourages social mobility and the mixture of castes. He explains how Ethiopian slaves often enter into slavery voluntarily and become members of their owners' families. In fact the offspring of slaves and their owners are free and treated "in all respects" like legal members of the family. In this sense, Ethiopian slavery blurs the distinction between personal and public spheres, between family and employee. This admixture, furthermore, brings with it the possibility for social mobility. Rogers's articulation of Ethiopian slavery transmutes a problematic component of Ethiopian culture into evidence of Ethiopia's lack of pure, static social categories. Moreover, his characterization of slavery contrasts with America's past and present exploitation of labor. Ethiopian slavery is more humane than American chattel slavery in the nineteenth century. Rogers compares slavery in Ethiopia to the experience of racialized labor in the context of Western imperialism: "But if we are inclined to be impatient with slavery in Ethiopia, let us remember that although it was abolished in America seventy years ago . . . [it] survives as peonage in the United States today. . . . Peonage in America is not only more harsh than slavery in Arabia and Ethiopia, but there is far less justification for it."

This passage deploys the Ethiopian labor practices as a frame to critique U.S. labor practices, but it also demonstrates the associative logic that underwrites the text's articulation of Afro-Diasporic solidarity as a whole. Rogers's treatment of Ethiopian slavery clearly illustrates his preference for practice over principle, induction over deduction. He argues that, although officially Ethiopia practices slavery, in actuality Ethiopian slavery is much more progressive than labor relations perpetuated by Western imperialism. His dissociation of slavery in name from actually existing inequity relies on an inductive privileging of experience over deductive generalizations. Thus the imposition of the general category "slavery" upon Ethiopian labor relations is akin to the application of racial categories to black experience in a domestic context. Indicting Ethiopian "slavery" is as superficial as policing "black and white." In contrast, Rogers's inductive approach observes commonalities between the experiences of contemporary raced labor and the practices of slavery in America's past.[45]

Through visual images of Ethiopians and inductive analysis of Ethiopian slavery, the text depicts Ethiopia as fundamentally heterogeneous and free of the static social categories that structure life within the states created by Western imperialism. The text further dissociates "Ethiopia" from Western imperialism by articulating a secular mythology that elides Ethiopia's geographic and political boundaries. In so doing, it substitutes rhetorical time for state borders as the ground of political community.

In a section titled "Geography, Economic Conditions, etc.," Rogers describes Ethiopian physical geography and natural resources. He states that the country's only border is a desert and that its climate is "heavenly"; Ethiopia has gorges larger than the Grand Canyon and mountains so high that it has been rightly called "The Switzerland of Africa"; and, as the source of gold for ancient Egypt, Ethiopia's natives "still wash gold in the same streams five thousand years later." Nature exists in extremes: the lion "attains its largest size there" and "the Ethiopian giraffe is among the tallest and finest in the world," while Ethiopia's temperature can reach a remarkable "150 degrees in the shade." These comparisons seem to suggest imperial appreciations of the preternatural fecundity of colonized space. Indeed, the language of origin explicitly echoes the rhetoric of cultural diffusion, a relationship Rogers seems to acknowledge when he writes that "Ethiopia was generally believed by the most ancient of scholars to have been the first of nations and the mother of civilization." However, his description of Ethiopian geography differs in that it characterizes the Ethiopian people as human actors in this space, not as mere reflections of the physical geography or as resources themselves.

Rogers compares the Italian and Ethiopian diplomacy that led up to the crisis and argues that, despite Italian complaints of Ethiopian perfidy, "The simple truth is that there has been no faith involved on either side. It was a case of ruse against ruse with the Africans being the trickier of the two"; thus his description in no way compromises Ethiopian agency. Indeed, his depiction of Ethiopian political behavior suggests that political acumen is common coin and has no space from which to diffuse and no essential connection to Western civilization. Moreover, Rogers's writing on Ethiopia actually tropes on colonial modes of writing. Rather than identifying essential racial and cultural distinctiveness, Rogers's "objective" perspective on Ethiopia actually denies the possibility of objective description. His archaeology unearths contemporaneousness; his ethnography of the "other" is explicitly *auto*ethnographic.[46]

Rogers's description of Ethiopia also elides its political borders by suggesting that the country could, in a sense, be experienced anywhere. For example, the pamphlet tells the story of Haile Selassie's life through an appropriation of the life of Christ set in Ethiopia. His life is related as a series of learning experiences and challenges that developed according to his destiny. In his youth he "nearly lost his life" when, "while crossing Lake Arumuya with seven others the boat capsized. He swam ashore; the rest were drowned." In this story young Ras Tafari could, in effect, walk on water when confronted with an experience that killed seven mortals. As "King of Kings of Ethiopia" Selassie also described as struggling with his own Pharisees. He fought against the "swarming Ethiopian clergy, which is very powerful, and ultra-conservative, and eager to keep the people in ignorance to serve its own ends." Last, his body exemplified humility. He "is barely over five feet tall, and weighs, it seems, not over a hundred and twenty pounds," and in his "general expression he has been aptly described by one writer as a 'black edition of the pictured Christ.'" In Rogers's narrative, Haile Selassie fulfills his destiny by maturing into a Christ-like king, and the space of Ethiopia is seen as the site of a time-bending repetition of the birth and growth of Christ, a spiritual space coincident with the ancient holy sites of the Levant *and* present contexts in which the undeserving must endure tribulation.[47]

Significantly, Rogers argues for a common black identity grounded not in a shared promise of redemption but in present political conditions, not in hope for tomorrow but in struggle today. Thus an Ethiopian state of mind is possible outside the borders of the Ethiopian state. "Ethiopian" is an identification that can be experienced in diverse political states within the larger context of modernity. Indeed, an Ethiopian state of mind transcends state borders and develops within the struggle against bureaucratic power, against authority that retards the development of human potential. The political nature of this coincidence signals a departure from the language of Christian redemptionism that had structured the early discourse of Ethiopianism. Nineteenth-century Ethiopianism situated Ethiopia in a Christian teleology wherein it was either to be redeemed or to be the source from which redemption would diffuse. Essentially, in Rogers's formulation, "Ethiopia" secularizes and politicizes the cultural work of the Ethiopianist tradition. Distanced from the colonial, diffusionist assumptions of the language of Christian redemptionism, the secular mythology of Ethiopia that emerges in response to the Italian invasion derives from a shared political condition. In Rogers's anticolonial vision, Ethiopia retains its mythic stature, but its metaphysical character has been displaced by political considerations. Indeed, this rhetoric replaces a Christian teleology with a material one.

Ultimately, in *The Real Facts about Ethiopia,* Ethiopia is a time and not a place. Ethiopia is now, a present, a moment in which those who share in exploitation also share in the potential to make change through purposeful action. As the foreword to the pamphlet argues, for the past four hundred centuries "the European, or white race, has been colonizing in all the lands of the darker races," and "for centuries this animosity has slumbered like a volcano, bursting at times into revenge as in the attacks on missionaries; the Indian mutiny; or the Zulu uprising."[48] Walter White, president of the NAACP, expressed a similar belief, claiming, "Italy, brazenly, has set fire under the powder keg of white arrogance and greed which seems to be an act of suicide for the so-called white world."[49] Now, however, is the time the cyclical disposition of power in history will complete its revolution.

Characterized in this fashion, the global political scene is a place of impending and inevitable crisis. Moreover, the forecast conflagration was preordained by the ancient actions of the forces of colonialization. The white European world sealed its fate, its downfall, and the eventual unification and uprising of the "colored" people of the world by its initiation of the Atlantic slave trade and subsequent colonial practices. This construction conjoins the slave trade outlawed in 1808, racist practices like lynching still practiced domestically, and the continuing international economic program of imperialism. The distant racist work of colonialism in foreign countries is immediate, a part of a repeating cycle of oppression and redemption materialized in the present moment.[50]

Rhetoric, Time, and Community

Rogers's mythological Ethiopia creates a frame for the performance of black community without the political borders of the United States;

"Ethiopia" orients people of African descent in time, providing a context in which to view the self in relation to others, the past, and the future. In this sense, Ethiopia functions as what Pierre Nora calls a *lieu de mémoire*.[51]

Lieu de mémoire is translated as a "realm," "site," or "place" of memory, though this formulation of public memory has little to do with an empirically verifiable past. In contrast with history, which is narrative and intellectual, a recollection of things that no longer exist, *lieux de mémoire* are lived, metaphorical, affective, and material. Memory, in this sense "takes root in the concrete, in spaces, gestures, images, and objects," while "history binds itself strictly to temporal continuities, to progressions."[52] *Lieux de mémoire* are outside the totalizing vision of history—they contradict history's linearity and purchase on the real. A moment of silence at a baseball game, for example, functions as a realm of memory in that it disrupts the narrative progression of time, creating a now that includes both past and future. In this sense, this performance of memory also establishes and orients community. Memory is *"political gestus,"* that is, "not just memory of past events, but memory of the future in anticipation of action to come."[53]

The *Lieux de memoire* concept has been used to explain the commemoration of space in black American expressive traditions.[54] Elizabeth Rauh Bethel argues that "Hayti" functioned as an African American *lieu de mémoire* in the nineteenth century. As Haiti's symbolic currency grew in black communities through emigration and the circulation of "myths" about the Haitian revolution, black Americans increasingly saw narratives of Haiti's past as constitutive elements of black experience in the United States.[55]

The circulation of *The Real Facts about Ethiopia* in black urban centers during the Great Depression constituted a progressive, Afro-Diasporic *lieu de mémoire*. Celebrating "Ethiopia" as a heterogeneous, borderless present, the text allowed for the rehearsal of pre-Diasporic black unity (*without* reliance on an empirically verifiable past). Through the lens of the Ethiopian *lieu de mémoire,* four hundred years of slavery, the contemporary fact of Jim Crow, and European occupation of Africa were constituted as repetitions of the fundamental spirit of a Western civilization, a spirit in decline. Moreover, domestic segregated public spaces themselves were presented as reifying the identification of the community and the position of that identity in a vision of history. With this present Ethiopian community in mind, an everyday racist act became proof of the transitional nature of racism and the eventuality of political change. Thus, this construction of Ethiopia as a foundational space provided a political explanation for present hardship and implied agency for intervention in domestic and international institutions.

The Politics of Black Anticolonialism

This analysis of Rogers's rhetoric explains how the fight against European imperialism in Ethiopia was perceived as a local event by many people of African descent. Ethiopia was not the center or origin of black political agency; rather, it was one of many equal fronts in the African Diaspora's struggle against colonialism and racism. The attitude toward black identity expressed in this text influenced black America's political culture at the close of the 1930s.

In 1934, the Ethiopian Research Council formed to disseminate information about Ethiopia's relevance to African America. As tensions with Italy increased, its politics became more aggressive, and eventually the organization became one of the focal points of African American agitation on behalf of Ethiopia. Supported by Haile Selassie, it also solicited economic support for the Ethiopian government. It eventually would give birth to a number of organizations that advocated radical action on behalf of Ethiopia on the street corners of Harlem and in black newspapers throughout the country's urban centers. The International Black League, the Afro-American Producers and Consumers League, the Ethiopian Guild of the Latter Day Garveyites, and Samuel Daniels's Pan African Reconstruction Association (PARA) lobbied for a radical approach to foreign and domestic racial politics that included boycotting Italian American businesses, patronizing black American businesses, and militarizing the struggle for black power.

The International African Progressive Association of Beckley, West Virginia, wrote to the secretary of state in 1935, "The black man in America is not an alien in any state or district anywhere in Africa, he was simply taken away against his will" and continued, "our emperor Haile Selassie is calling upon the descendants of the very Africans who were seized and brought to this country by violence; the insistent call of Africans at home must be answered by Africans abroad."[56] Perhaps the most vivid instance of the enactment of this Afro-diasporic community occurred on June 26, 1936, when the "Brown Bomber" Joe Louis fought

"Mussolini's Darling," Italian Primo Carnera, at Yankee Stadium. Louis knocked out the much larger Italian in the sixth round, and even though Louis was from Detroit, his victory provided ground for African American identification with the mythic indomitability of the diminutive state of Ethiopia in its fight against heavily favored Italy. After Louis's victory, black people could believe that "Ethiopia's army could march into Rome and lick the Italians with their natural fists." As reported in the *New York Times* the following day, a PARA meeting on July 14, 1935, began with the Reverend Harold Williamson asking attendees to "get right up and tell why we want to knock out Mussolini like Joe Louis did Carnera." One man responded to Williams's provocation: "I don't see why Ethiopia should be just another nation of slaves for the white man. An' I'll fight for Ethiopia an' give my life an' blood."[57]

The Italian invasion of Ethiopia was a seminal moment in black American rhetorical history, a powerful moment of consensus and political activism. Writing in the *Pittsburgh Courier,* George Schuyler noted that he had not met a single black person in the United States who did not want to help the Ethiopian people: "the colored people were intensely interested in the struggle and burning to do their little bit to aid the largest independent colored nation in the world."[58]

Ultimately, the Italian invasion of Ethiopia inspired the expression of an Afro-Diasporic community empowered to respond to colonialism and racism in Africa and in the United States. J. A. Rogers's *The Real Facts about Ethiopia* critiqued colonialism as the imposition of discrete cultural spaces on complex, fluid experience. It suggested that racial categories and political boundaries were capricious and perpetuated class-based oppression. In contrast, race in its universal sense, was truer, complex, hybrid, and grounded in the experience of difference. The sense of Ethiopian solidarity that emerged in response to the Italian invasion of Ethiopia expressed consubstantiality with the African Diaspora that did not require the negation of ontological difference. In this sense, through a politicized temporal frame, black Americans could perceive a shared political condition and motivation, indeed a shared sense of political identity, without dislodging Ethiopia or black America's cultural and existential particularity.

J. A. Rogers's *The Real Facts about Ethiopia* demonstrates the maturation of the rhetorical processes through which the African Diaspora became a political concept in the 1930s. The text critiques the creation of political borders and the maintenance of discrete cultural spaces,

CHAPTER 5

creating a mythology of an alternative, global context for subject formation. Rogers employs rhetorical time and the performance of memory to constitute the African Diaspora as a public empowered to confront international colonialism and domestic racial politics. This rhetoric illustrates a sense of political community that is not coextensive with the state. Still, the opposition between stateless and state community does not obviate the political character of the African Diaspora, nor is it evidence of the absence of political authority. The African Diaspora is not merely a cultural entity. Rather, in texts like Joel A. Rogers's *The Real Facts about Ethiopia* the African Diaspora is a political community with the agency to contest state power both in general and in the form of specific policies.

European, fascist aggression against an independent African and Christian nation was a poignant dramatization of the political and economic tensions being experienced by black people in diaspora. When Ethiopian sovereignty was endangered, "Afro-Americans put a most inspired and concerted agitation for African freedom and independence, and raised African consciousness to a point where it became a force in the world."[59] This new consciousness appeared in public protest and argument in diverse regions of the country, by individuals and organizations of various backgrounds. Indeed, it also allowed for increased political coordination within the diverse cultures of the African Diaspora. As black Americans protested against Italian imperialism, with the same voice they protested against domestic racism. Black American anticolonialism was a reciprocal, local event in a global contest.

CHAPTER 6

Anticolonial Rhetoric and Black Civil Rights History

I N 1935, SAMUEL DANIELS, founder of the Pan-African Reconstruction Association and a prominent Harlem race advocate, suggested that Haiti, Liberia, and Ethiopia should unite and form a single corporation. He reasoned that this economic conglomerate could compete with European imperialism and establish a transnational base of "African" political power. Although the idea may seem fanciful, even utopian, Daniels's vision of African-Diasporic community was complex; his plan for a Pan-African, anticolonial corporation was motivated by a need for economic self-defense and thus gave the lie to the putative altruism that justified European imperialism. Also, although Daniels was attempting to shift the focus of international commerce from the West, like nineteenth-century nationalists Martin Delaney and Robert Campbell who sought an African epicenter for black collective identity, his foundation for black power was as dispersed as the diaspora itself. Departing from his predecessors, Daniels did not suggest a single geographic center for black economic and political power but an arrangement between communities with shared interests. Finally, the corporate model he chose suggests his dissatisfaction with the state as an organizing principle for political community. He preferred incorporation over nationalism, desiring to coordinate rather than assimilate the cultures of the African Diaspora, and in so doing expressed his skepticism about the state and optimism about new forms of black collective identity.[1]

Obviously, Daniels's Africa, Inc. never came about. But Daniels, like other black anticolonialists during the 1930s, participated in a powerful new rhetoric, a transformation in black ethos that challenged white supremacy, proposed innovative relationships within the African Diaspora, and put forth possible models of progressive black community.

A coherent black ethos developed through the medium of black anti-colonial rhetoric as it interpreted the U.S. occupation of Haiti, the Liberian labor crisis, and the Italian invasion of Ethiopia. The rhetoric of this black collective identity differed from much of the discourse that had preceded it. Prior rhetorics of black community were implicated in cultural nationalism and, like European nationalism, emerged from the politics and practices of colonialism; cultural diffusion — the belief that cultural and racial groups existed at the core or on the periphery of world historical narratives — shaped the rhetoric that expressed collective identity. Modern nationalism, and indeed the modern subject of the Enlightenment, came into being through managing commerce between these distinct cultural spaces: the metropolitan and the periphery, civilized and primitive, autonomous and dependent. People of African descent confronted, configured, and conformed to these assumptions in rhetoric that imagined and mobilized transnational political community.

In the early years of the twentieth century, when people of African descent argued against racist policies they often invented new frameworks for viewing their experience. The highly influential Pan-African rhetoric of W. E. B. Du Bois and Marcus Garvey used African spaces as metaphors for reconstituted black identity or as benchmarks for the evolution of black culture. Ultimately, this rhetoric served an existential function for black people in that it created an ontological center to bring together disparate African ethnicities and to disprove ideologies of racial inferiority through the sharing of a common metaphysical substance (the "race," its destiny, or a debt to a sense of civilization, for example). These interpretations of Africa and the international diaspora served to buttress or recuperate black American existence, to stabilize black being rather than articulate a specific political community within which to contest specific policies. Indeed, this rhetoric required the recognition of distinct political circumstances among Africans, African Americans, and the African Diaspora as a condition for commonality among the people of these places. Ultimately, this rhetoric posited an epistemological subject as the foundation for political agency. It assumed the desirability of a single, unproblematic focal point as the font of political agency within the African Diaspora.

Through their responses to colonialist actions in Haiti, Liberia, and Ethiopia, black people were able to imagine a new sense of political community, a black ethos not defined by state boundaries or a single focal point. This community rejected the political borders created and maintained by white supremacy, but it did not eschew the imaginative political borders of black community. In this sense, while this discourse is Pan-African, it does not rely on the language of return or on the idea that Africa is a homeland for black people in diaspora. From this perspective, black people are at home in America, but they are also at home in Africa, Europe, and the West Indies.

This anticolonial rhetoric expressed what Stuart Hall calls a "Diasporic" sense of self and community. According to Hall, a diaspora is defined, "not by essence or purity, but by the recognition of a necessary heterogeneity and diversity; by a conception of 'identity' which lives with and through, not despite, difference; by *hybridity*. Diaspora identities are those which are constantly producing and reproducing themselves anew, through transformation and difference."[2] Diaspora, in Hall's formulation, then, promises a shift from traditional fonts of political authority; unlike a state, an international diaspora does not have a military or the ability to tax, and it cannot participate in electoral politics as would a political party. However, although Hall views diaspora as a cultural phenomenon, as this book demonstrates, diasporic community is equally political, and speaking from diaspora is one way to exercise influence in the traditional spaces of political power. Indeed, the sense of black ethos and African Diasporic community that emerged in black anticolonial rhetoric during the Great Depression expands our understanding of the relationship between cultural and political modes of collective symbolic action. In its immediate context, this rhetoric was progressive in a number of ways: it utilized the language of colonialism to expose and critique white supremacy, provided innovative approaches to domestic political action, and created a forum for the negotiation and mobilization of Black Nationalist sentiment.

Black anticolonialism during the 1930s attacked white supremacy by interrogating colonialism and exposing how domestic racial politics influenced U.S. foreign policy in particular. It also debunked the language of sacrifice and benign paternalism that had been used to justify U.S. colonial endeavors. Popular rhetoric discussed U.S. foreign policy in moral terms; black anticolonialism excavated the economic imperatives and self-interest that underlay many of these policies. In this sense, the critique also undermined the rhetoric of American exceptionalism that emerged from justifications of American imperialism. This rhetoric exposed the actual avarice and violence inherent in colonial practices and thus contributed to a critical perspective on the administration of the American empire.

Another result of the black anticolonialist critique was the historicizing and contextualization of the performance of race, and thus disruption of the hegemony of emerging rhetorics of "whiteness." In the wake of World War I, popular texts argued for Americanism, nativism, and white supremacy. Madison Grant, for example, lamented that the First World War and the increasing solidarity of the world's not-so-white populations were evidence of an impending conflagration that would end European hegemony.[3] Black anticolonialism diagnosed the polarization of the globe in terms favorable to the African Diaspora, choosing black interests as the frame of reference for understanding changes in global politics, culture, and economics. In so doing, black anticolonial rhetoric participated in the representation of race, in giving expression, value, and truth to racial community. Black race making is significant because black people were themselves "colonized" or, more accurately, were constituted in a field of discourse that tried to circumvent their power to "create" racial community.

Stephanie Baptiste explored tensions within this representational function in black American discourse through her analysis of the rhetoric of primitivism in the 1936 and 1938 theatrical productions "Voodoo Macbeth" and "Haiti." There, Baptiste argues that representing an "other" is basic to the dynamics of power, desire, and the discourse of nation within modernity. Therefore, black American primitivist representations of the Diaspora in these two plays evidence black American modernism.[4] She also pointed out that black American primitivists during the Great Depression exercised cultural power through their representations of a diasporic "other." In her haste to recuperate primitivism and discover black American agency, however, Baptiste neglects how this "othering" in context also achieves a self-othering and disarticulation of the African Diaspora. As the texts considered in this book demonstrate, a second discourse of diaspora existed during this period. Black American anticolonialism, in departing from the discourses of *both* colonialism *and* primitivism, was a corollary and perhaps more progressive expression of black modernity. Rather than repeating exotic representations of the African Diaspora, black anticolonialists reconfigured the possible meaning of the "exotic." They emphasized the hybrid nature of identity and resituated the performance of self and culture within a global context. In this larger frame, cultural particularity became constitutive of political community: it was neither forgotten nor commoditized.

The rhetoric that evolved during this period provided impetus to political organization, innovative ways of approaching domestic racial politics, and new articulations of domestic political agency. In the 1930s anticolonialism created a common ground for diverse black organizations dedicated to both international and domestic progress and to exploring possible relationships between these two dimensions of progressive politics. Black organizations once in tension found an imperative and common cause in opposing European imperialism.

African and Caribbean ex-patriots living in black America's urban centers formed new organizations, and Western imperialism created exigencies for black American travel throughout the Diaspora, thus facilitating personal connections among individuals of African descent. For example, James Weldon Johnson assisted in the formation of the Haitian nationalist organization, the Union Patriotique, in Harlem. The Union Patriotique lobbied against the U.S. occupation and disseminated information about Haiti and the occupation through formal and informal networks in Harlem. The Liberian Labor crisis facilitated U.S. visits from Americo-Liberian politicians and businessmen and travel to Liberia by black Americans like George Schuyler. The Italian invasion of Ethiopia inspired the "Black Eagle" Hubert Julian and the "Brown Condor" John Robinson to travel to Africa and interact with Africans of diverse economic and ethnic backgrounds. Julian's exploits in Africa were front-page news in black American newspapers. While in Africa, he formed relationships with Ethiopia's royalty and military, some of which continued after his return to the United States.[5]

As the Italian invasion of Ethiopia became an occupation, the conglomerate of organizations once formed for Ethiopia's defense focused their energies on domestic issues, and anticolonialism became the context for understanding domestic and foreign policy. The Ethiopian World Federation, for example, lobbied for federal antilynching legislation. In addition, many people of African descent spoke out against U.S. involvement in World War II and cited lessons learned from European colonialism in the 1930s as evidence of the perfidy of the West. Indeed, as David Aldridge argues, black people tended to view World War II through "an antiracist, anticolonial and Third World-centered foreign policy sensibility that made them view the Western democracies less benignly than many white Americans."[6] W. E. B. Du Bois, Roy Wilkins, and George Schuyler all sympathized with Axis Germany because it had attacked Britain and France, nations with more repugnant colonial regimes. Not until Pearl Harbor did many black people publicly denounce Japanese aggression; up to that point, they considered Japan a model "raced" nation, an anti-Western imperialism superpower. Anticolonial discourse was so powerful that ninety-eight black Americans traveled to Spain to participate in the Spanish Civil War, one of whom wrote in a letter home, "This ain't Ethiopia, but it'll do."[7]

Black anticolonial rhetoric during this period also supplied a forum in which anthropological discourse could be applied to foreign policy and domestic racial politics. Bishop Reverdy Ransom at Wilberforce, Ernest Work at Muskinghum, and William Leo Hansberry at Howard University each opposed colonialism through their academic studies of indigenous African culture. Hansberry was particularly prolific. His anthropologies of Africa and Ethiopia appeared in his expressions of agitation against the Italian invasion in the popular press.[8] These anthropological appreciations of the African Diaspora differed from prior academic focuses on Africa's ancient past, mythic personalities, or modern futures. Rather, this anthropology investigated the dynamics of contemporary African culture and was read by a mass audience. Most important, however, it also facilitated a rhetoric that emphasized rather than underplayed cultural difference in the service of political solidarity. Black anticolonialism neither forgot nor sensationalized the foreign characteristics of African cultures: it accentuated their cultural particularity; explained them through the discursive frames of anthropology, history, and political economy; and managed the exotic through arguing for coordinate political community.

Ultimately, through their responses to colonial violence in the 1930s, black Americans demonstrated a sense of political agency in which domestic black culture shifted from a synecdochical to a metonymical relationship with the cultures of the African Diaspora. No longer a derivative or an exemplary "part of a whole" glorious African past or future, this rhetoric cast black people in diaspora as coordinate with Africans enduring colonialism anywhere in the world. In this sense, black anticolonialism transformed a sentiment about the relationship between black Americans and the African Diaspora into a "people" as a political concept. Historian James Meriwether argues that this sense of a symmetrical African Diaspora emerged in tandem with post–World War II African independence movements and reached its maturity in the 1960s. Meriwether's correlation of black anticolonialism and African Diasporic nationalism contributes an international frame of reference to domestic civil rights rhetoric, but the rhetoric of black anticolonialists in the 1930s demonstrates an earlier moment of genesis for Afro-Diasporic nationalism and for the authority of anticolonialism in critiques of domestic racial politics.[9]

Black anticolonialism in the 1930s also provided a space for the expression of political arguments and organizations that were distinctly black. Following August Meir and Elliot Rudwick, Celeste Condit and John Lucaites have suggested that Black Nationalism was largely dormant from the decline of Garvey in the mid-1920s until its resurgence in the mid- to late 1960s.[10] This was not the case. Although many of Garvey's erstwhile followers enlisted in the decidedly antinationalist religious communities of Father Divine and Daddy Grace, the significance and popularity of distinct and authentic black political space did not diminish during this period.[11] Rather, black anticolonialism provided a space for increased debate about the scope and characteristics of distinctly black community in an international context. Indeed, the idea of a distinctly black community was a lively and vibrant factor in black American life long after Garvey and long before Malcolm X. A variety of Black Nationalist sentiment endured in the rhetoric and activism of anticolonial organizations in the late thirties. For example, in August 1937 one of the premier anticolonial groups of that period, United Aid for Ethiopia, was dissolved because many of its members thought the group had been contaminated by Communists. This reorganization suggested a commitment among some black people to the notion that authentic black interests were best served by organizations devoted exclusively to black politics. The new organization, Ethiopian World Federation, was all black and devoted to the needs of an Afro-Diasporic community. The organization published *The Voice of Ethiopia,* a Harlem newspaper for the "Vast Universal Black Commonwealth," in 1937. Eventually, the paper was also distributed in other black urban areas, and it enlisted locals to serve as correspondents.

Although the paper agitated against colonialism in Ethiopia, it devoted the bulk of its pages to contesting the legacy and "racial attachment" of Marcus Garvey for his recantation of his earlier, enthusiastic support of the Ethiopian cause. When Italy was preparing to invade Ethiopia, Garvey had praised Haile Selassie and ranted against the "smell" of "the brute" Mussolini.[12] In 1937, however, he castigated Selassie, claiming in the *Negro World* that he had "kept his country unprepared for modern civilization . . . he resorted sentimentally to prayer and to feasting and to fasting, not consistent with the policy that secures the existence of present day freedom for peoples while other nations and rulers are building up armaments of the most destructive kind as the only means of securing peace."[13] Garvey's later criticism of Selassie was interpreted by many as evidence of an absence of an "authentic" commitment to the race.[14]

Garvey's statement and the response it generated demonstrate how moments of Western imperialism were an opportunity to debate the parameters of blackness, the political interests of black people, and the role of the "authentic" in both. Equally important, the popular and complex nature of this anticolonial rhetoric provided a space for negotiating black authenticity. Unlike the Garvey movement, which despite its calls for Pan-African community often inspired anti-Caribbean aggression in black American urban communities, black anticolonialism in the 1930s argued for a collective black community in which black Americans, West Indians, and Africans of diverse economic backgrounds would figure and have equal voice.[15]

In some ways, however, black American anticolonialism in the 1930s also struggled with many of the issues that have continually plagued distinctly black collective identity. Assertions of Afro-Diasporic solidarity were coopted by racial regressives like Senator Theodore Bilbo, who in 1939 proposed a repatriation scheme designed to eliminate black America from U.S. democracy.[16]

In the early 1940s black anticolonial rhetoric became more generally internationalist in scope. By and large, during that decade black anticolonialists shifted their focus from African Diasporic activism to an activism that advocated human rights more generally. In the United States, the black voice on foreign policy had traditionally had a Pan-African or Black Nationalist accent, but in the 1940s, according to Brenda Gayle Plummer, these "enthusiasms were at a low ebb."[17] For example, black leaders like Ralph Bunche and Walter White argued that the 1945 Pan-African Conference should avoid Pan-Africanism altogether and lobbied to change its name to the "World Races Conference" or the "Conference on Colonial Problems."[18]

After 1947, protest on behalf of colonial peoples, expressions of international racial solidarity, and references to universal white oppression decreased even more, being replaced by domestic political action. Most black leaders narrowed their focus, fighting for civil rights within the boundaries of their own states and employing the language of political liberalism.[19] Indeed, by the "end of the 1940s, beyond a broad concern about colonialism, few strong ties existed between black America and contemporary Africa."[20] This shift in emphasis can be explained in a number of ways — among them internecine conflict between black political organizations, economic progress in black communities, and the perception that the Truman administration was committed to some degree of social change. But the primary force acting on this rhetoric was the context of the Cold War, which created a particular crisis in black internationalism and problematized black anticolonial rhetoric.

More specifically, during the Cold War, movements for self-determination in Africa and elsewhere and the nationalist rhetoric that motivated these movements were easily construed as not sufficiently anti-Communist and thus potentially sympathetic to Communism's designs.[21] Despite the promise of the Atlantic Charter that World War II had been fought ostensibly to promote "self-rule," postwar U.S. policies like the Marshall Plan allowed European powers to retain their colonial possessions. Thus anticolonialism was a casualty of an anti-Communism that preferred stable colonies to potential victims of Soviet expansionism.[22] For instance, despite his sympathy for colonized people and his commitment to decolonization, Secretary of State John Foster Dulles cautioned restraint, because he believed too rapid decolonization might produce in colonial states a "captivity far worse than present dependence."[23] This argument — that colonized people around the globe should surrender their independence in order to enjoy the protection of the modern, democratic antagonist in the Cold War — merely replicated the paternalism of colonialists and of progressive black leaders like members of the NAACP and participants in the Pan-African Congresses who advocated a form of trusteeship for states undergoing decolonization. In the early years of the 1950s, black anticolonial rhetoric lost its power credibly to articulate a distinct black experience and to motivate activism throughout the African Diaspora. Moreover, politicians like Secretary of State Dulles increasingly employed a liberal discourse about Africa and colonized nations that regenerated the paternal assumptions of colonial discourse.

And yet, in 1947 the government of Liberia named Missouri native Melvin B. Tolson its poet laureate. In this role, Tolson's charge was to compose a poem commemorating the one hundredth anniversary of Liberian statehood. Tolson claimed that the poem he finished in 1953, *The Libretto for the Republic of Liberia,* was inspired by George Schuyler's *Slaves Today: A Story of Liberia.* Clearly, the poem is also a response to modernity. Labyrinthine in complexity, rife with paradox and annotation, the poem satirizes T. S. Eliot's *The Wasteland;* but *The Libretto* finds support for its poetic argument in the late 1930s work of Joel Augustus Rogers and W. E. B. Du Bois.[24]

The poem tells the epic tale of Liberia's history, present and future. But the Liberia it describes is a sensibility and an attitude toward modernity rather than a state or demarcated physical geography. The poem argues that people of African descent form a coherent collective identity, not because of phenotype, a single destiny, or their common debt to an ancient past, but because of their common history with colonialism and a shared political condition within modernity.

Although the poem characterizes Liberia as an essential actor in modernity, it is in no sense a pure point of origin from which "civilization" spread or evolved. The poem avoids mythologizing Liberia's origin and offering an apology for its present. For example, one section of the poem poetically represents the negotiations that secured resources for African Americans to travel to West Africa and found the Liberian state. The poem states that "Old Robert Finley" managed to "pinion Henry Clay, the shuttlecock" and establish an organization to fund African American colonization of Africa, the American Colonization Society.[25] In Tolson's retelling, Liberia's founding was, in a sense, political rather than moral or mythological; Liberia began with an act of political will, the pursuit of a self-interest shared by black people around the globe.

Tolson's poem demonstrates the enduring significance of the black anticolonial rhetoric of the 1930s. Long after the Great Depression, the arguments of black anticolonialists continued to influence how people of African descent talked about international black community. Poets like Melvin Tolson, and later Stephen Henderson and Amiri Baraka, discovered a rhetorical resource in the anticolonial rhetoric of the 1930s, a field of arguments and tropes for characterizing international black community. Activists like Robert Williams, founder of the Revolutionary Action Movement, and Malcolm X visited this rhetoric as well, discovering inspiration and models for their political programs.[26]

In 1938, George S. Schuyler published a series of short stories in the *Pittsburgh Courier.* The stories told of a unique black genius, Dr. Belsidus, who, through a combination of political cunning and great intellect, united the African Diaspora and waged a successful war against the West.[27] When published, the stories were titled "Black Empire," but their original title, "Black Belt Millennium," is, in retrospect, more appropriate in conveying the attitude toward the African Diaspora that thrived during the 1930s. Schuyler's stories forecast the rise of black political power to confront Western imperialism, an agency that emerged from a "black belt" that circled the globe.

NOTES

Introduction: Rhetoric and Diaspora

1. Steven Watson, *The Harlem Renaissance: Hub of African American Culture* (New York: Pantheon Books, 1995).

2. Houston Baker, *Modernism and the Harlem Renaissance* (Chicago: University of Chicago Press, 1987), 85; Bruce Tyler, *From Harlem to Hollywood: The Struggle for Racial and Cultural Democracy, 1920–1943* (New York: Garland, 1992), 13.

3. Originally published in Cullen's 1925 book *Color,* the version that appears in *The New Negro* was substantially edited and truncated, likely by Locke himself. See James Kelly, "Blossoming in Strange New Forms: Male Homosexuality and the Harlem Renaissance," *Soundings: An Interdisciplinary Journal* 80.4 (Winter 1997): 498–517.

4. Countee Cullen, "Heritage," in *The New Negro,* ed. Alain Locke (New York: Simon & Schuster, 1925), 250.

5. Melvin Dixon, "The Black Writer's Use of Memory," in *History and Memory in African American Culture,* ed. Robert O'Meally and Genevieve Fabre (Oxford: Oxford University Press, 1994), 23–4.

6. David Levering Lewis, *When Harlem Was in Vogue* (New York: Penguin, 1997).

7. Steven Mailloux, *Reception Histories: Rhetoric, Pragmatism, and American Cultural Politics* (Ithaca, N.Y.: Cornell University Press, 1998).

8. Robert Carr, *Black Nationalism in the New World* (Chapel Hill, N.C.: Duke University Press, 2002).

9. For a brief but insightful treatment of how characterizations of Africa have mattered in New World black subjectivity, see Mary Louise Pratt, "Scratches on the Face of the Country, or What Mr. Barrow Saw in the Land of the Bushman," in *Race Writing and Difference,* ed. Henry Louis Gates, Jr. (Chicago: Chicago University Press, 1986), 138–62; Marianna Torgovnick, *Gone Primitive: Savage Intellects, Modern Lives* (Chicago: University of Chicago Press, 1990); Sieglinde Lemke, *Primitivist Modernism: Black Culture and the Origins of the Transatlantic Modernism* (Oxford: Oxford University Press, 1998).

10. Alfred W. Hunt, *Haiti's Influence on Antebellum America* (Baton Rouge: Louisiana State University Press, 1988).

11. David Walker, *David Walker's Appeal* (New York: Hill & Wang, 1995), 93.

12. James Hall, *An Address to the Free People of Color of the State of Maryland* (Baltimore: John D. Troy, 1859).

13. For further explanation of the symbolic importance of the Haitian Revolution in black and white American discourse see, Sibylle Fischer, *Modernity Disavowed: Haiti and the Culture of Slavery in the Age of Revolution* (Chapel Hill, N.C.: Duke University Press, 2004).; Elizabeth Rauh Bethel, "Images of Hayti: The Construction of an Afro-American Lieu de Memoire," *Callaloo* 15.3 (1992): 827–41; Bruce Dain, "Haiti and Egypt in Early Black Racial Discourse in the United States," *Slavery and Abolition* 14.3 (1993): 139–61. Chris Dixon, *African America and Haiti: Emigration and Black Nationalism in the Nineteenth Century* (Westport, Conn.: Greenwood Press, 2000).

14. Cited in Dorothy Porter, ed., *Early Negro Writing, 1760–1837* (Boston: Beacon, 1971).

15. For a discussion of the academic emergence of the term "Diaspora" and its attendant assumptions, see Brent Hayes Edwards, "The Uses of Diaspora," *Social Text* 19.1 (2001): 45–73. The term "diaspora" did not commonly describe Africans and African cultures outside the African continent until the 1960s. Since the 1960s "diaspora" has served a number of scholarly enterprises. James Clifford surveys a number of these contemporary theoretical constructions of the term and, roughly, argues that "diaspora" describes a transnational community defined by a feeling of displacement, melancholia, and resistance. He departs from the assumption that a diaspora is defined by its dispersal. Instead, he describes it as having two simultaneous modes, vertical (the language of return) and lateral (a decentered, shared sense of suffering). However, Clifford's explicit and implicit use of the language of melancholy creates too restrictive a definition of diaspora. This definition excludes communities that bring nuance to the term, like some contemporary Zionist organizations and the black anticolonial rhetoric under study in this project that find in Diaspora a source of political agency and optimism. Indeed, most contemporary scholarly work that develops or employs the concept "diaspora" theorizes cultural dynamics to the neglect of the political mobilization of diasporic community. James Clifford, "Diasporas," *Cultural Anthropology* 9.3 (1994): 302–38.

16. Drake's seminal interpretation of black American political and cultural investment remains one of the most complete narratives of the relationship between black America and Africa. See St. Clair Drake, "Negro Americans and the Africa Interest," in *The American Negro Reference Book,* ed. John P. Davis (Englewood Cliffs, N.J.: Prentice-Hall, 1966), 662–705.

17. Stephen Howe, *Afrocentrism: Mythical Pasts and Imagined Homes* (New York: Verso, 1998).

18. Paul Gilroy, *The Black Atlantic: Modernity and Double Consciousness* (Cambridge, Mass.: Harvard University Press) 1993.

19. Brent Hayes Edwards, *The Practice of Diaspora: Literature, Translation, and Black Internationalism* (Cambridge, Mass.: Harvard University Press), 2003.

20. Michael Hanchard, "Translation, Political Community, and Black Internationalism: Some Comments on Brent Hayes Edwards' Practices of Diaspora," *Small Axe* 9.1 (2005): 112–19.

21. Kenneth Burke, *A Rhetoric of Motives* (Berkeley: University of California Press, 1950).

22. Michael Calvin McGee, "In Search of 'the People': A Rhetorical Alternative," *The Quarterly Journal of Speech* 61.3 (1975): 235–49.

23. Michael Calvin McGee, "In Search of 'the People,'" 244.

24. Ibid., 245.

25. Maurice Charland, "Constitutive Rhetoric: The Case of the *Peuple Quebecois*," *The Quarterly Journal of Speech* 73.2 (1987): 133–50.

26. Ibid., 133.

27. Ibid., 134.

28. For further explanation of social identity, see Craig Calhoun, "The Problem of Identity in Collective Action," in *Macro-Micro Linkages in Sociology*, ed. Joan Huber (Newbury Park, Calif.: Sage, 1991), 51–75.

29. New Social Movement theory is not without its detractors. In particular, scholars criticize the ostensible "newness" of New Social Movement activism and the theory's inability to explain conservative social movements. Still, the notion of collective identity is useful for rhetorical scholars because it focuses critical attention on the processes through which collectivities form. For a thorough critique of the New Social Movement paradigm, see Nelson Pichardo, "New Social Movements: A Critical Review," *Annual Review of Sociology* 23 (1997): 411–30.

30. Hank Johnston, Enrique Larana, and Joseph R. Gusfield, "Identities, Grievances, and New Social Movements," in *New Social Movements: From Ideology to Identity*, ed. Enrique Larana, Hank Johnston, and Joseph R. Gusfield (Philadelphia: Temple University Press, 1994): 3–35.

31. Alberto Melucci, "The Process of Collective Identity," in *Social Movements and Culture*, ed. Hank Johnston and Bert Klandermans (Minneapolis: University of Minnesota Press, 1995), 44.

32. Alberto Melucci, *Nomads of the Present: Social Movements and Individual Needs in Contemporary Society* (Philadelphia: Temple University Press, 1989), 35.

33. Rajagopalan Radhakrishnan, *Diasporic Mediations: Between Home and Location* (Minneapolis: University of Minnesota Press, 1996).

34. Martin Medhurst, "The Contemporary Study of Public Address: Renewal, Recovery, and Reconfiguration," *Rhetoric and Public Affairs* 4.3 (2001): 495–507.

35. Dexter Gordon, *Black Identity: Rhetoric, Ideology, and 19th Century Black Nationalism* (Carbondale: Southern Illinois University Press, 2006).

36. Amritjit Singh and Peter Schmidt, *Postcolonial Theory and the United States: Race, Ethnicity, and Literature* (Jackson: University Press of Mississippi, 2000).

37. Caroline Levander and Robert S. Levin, "Introduction: Hemispheric Literary History," *American Literary History* 18.3 (2006): 397–405.

38. Michelle Stephens, "Re-imagining the Shape and Borders of Black Political Space," *Radical History Review* 87 (2003): 169–82.

39. Michael Hanchard, "Afro-Modernity: Temporality, Politics, and the African Diaspora," *Public Culture* 11.1 (1999), 247–48.

40. Sibylle Fischer, *Modernity Disavowed: Haiti and the Culture of Slavery in the Age of Revolution* (Durham, N.C.: Duke University Press, 2004).

41. Ifeoma Kiddoe Nwankwo, *Black Cosmopolitanism: Racial Consciousness and Transnational Identity in the Nineteenth-Century Americas* (Philadelphia: University of Pennsylvania Press, 2005).

42. Cited in Elizabeth L. Normandy, "African-Americans and U.S. Policy Towards Liberia 1929–1935," *Liberian Studies Journal* 18.2 (1993): 203–30.

43. Alain Locke, "Slavery in the Modern Manner," *Survey,* March 31, 1931; W. E. B. Du Bois, "Postscript — Liberia," *Crisis,* March 1931.

1. The Politics and Practices of Colonialism

1. See Raka Shome, "Postcolonial Interventions in the Rhetorical Canon: An 'Other' View," *Communication Theory* 6 (1996): 40–59.

2. Abdul R. JanMohamed, "The Economy of Manichean Allegory: The Function of Racial Difference in Colonialist Literature," in *Race, Writing, and Difference,* ed. Henry Louis Gates Jr. (Chicago: University of Chicago Press), 80. Nicholas Thomas makes a similar plea for historical scholarship that investigates the phenomenon of colonialism through analysis of its situated practices. Nicholas Thomas, *Colonialism's Culture: Anthropology, Travel, and Government* (Princeton, N.J.: Princeton University Press, 1994).

3. R. Radhakrisnan, "Postcoloniality and the Boundaries of Identity," *Callaloo* 16.4 (1993): 764.

4. Blaut argues that colonialism and Eurocentrism are synonymous, and therefore colonialism began with the conceit of Columbus's "discovery." Others argue that colonialism refers only to European expansion from the end of the nineteenth century to the outbreak of World War I. As Laura Chrisman argues, even Spivak, Jameson, and Said, eminent theorists of modernity, disagree about the temporal boundaries of colonialism and imperialism. See J. M. Blaut, *The Colonizer's Model of the World* (New York: Guilford Press, 1993); Laura Chrisman, "Imperial Space, Imperial Place: Theories of Empire and Culture in Fredric Jameson, Edward Said, and Gayatri Spivak," *New Formations* 34 (1998): 53–69.

5. Patrick Williams and Laura Chrisman, "Colonial Discourse and Postcolonial Theory: An Introduction," in *Colonial Discourse and Post Colonial Theory: A Reader,* ed. Patrick Williams and Laura Chrisman (New York: Harvester Wheatsheaf, 1993), 2.

6. J. H. Parry, *The Age of Reconnaissance* (New York: New American Library, 1963).

7. Stephen Greenblatt, *Marvelous Possessions: The Wonder of the New World* (Chicago: University of Chicago Press); Mary Louise Pratt, *Imperial Eyes: Travel Writing and Acculturation* (New York: Routledge, 1992).

8. Blaut, *Colonizer's Model of the World.*

9. Johan Friedrich Blumenbach, *On the Natural Varieties of Mankind* (New York: Bergman, 1969).

10. Herder, one of the architects of German nationalism, was also very influential in the development of other nationalisms. Appiah contends that Black Nationalism inherited Herder's racist assumptions. Moses disagrees with Appiah, holding that Herder was not racist by the standard of his peers and pointing out that no direct evidence exists to support Appiah's thesis that Black Nationalism was derived from German nationalism. Rather, he argues, Black Nationalism was a "cognate" or "analogue" to German nationalism. This chapter follows Moses and explores the cultural and historical context that gave rise to both intellectual traditions. See Kwame Anthony Appiah, *My Father's House* (New York: Oxford University Press, 1999), 20; Wilson Jeremiah Moses, *Afrotopia: The Roots of African-American Popular History* (Cambridge: Cambridge University Press, 1998), 152.

11. K. R. Minogue, *Nationalism* (New York: Penguin, 1970); John H. Zammito, *Kant, Herder, and the Birth of Anthropology* (Chicago: University of Chicago Press, 2002).

12. Edward Said, *Orientalism* (New York: Vintage Books, 1994).

13. For further discussion of the scope and significance of intellectual labor in the emergence of the modern notion of race, see David Theo Goldberg, *Racist Culture: Philosophy and the Politics of Meaning* (Cambridge, Mass.: Blackwell, 1993).

14. Moses, *Afrotopia*.

15. Leopold II, cited in Adam Hochschild, *King Leopold's Ghost: A Story of Greed, Terror, and Heroism in Colonial Africa* (Boston: Houghton Mifflin, 1998), 44.

16. Thomas Pakenham, *The Scramble for Africa: The White Man's Conquest of the Dark Continent from 1876 to 1912* (New York: Random House, 1991).

17. For further detail about the emergence of colonialism and specific state practices, see Alice L. Conklin and Ian Christopher Fletcher, *European Imperialism, 1830–1930: Climax and Contradiction* (Boston: Houghton Mifflin, 1999); Anne Phillips, *The Enigma of Colonialism: British Policy in West Africa* (Bloomington: Indiana University Press, 1989).

18. Melvin E. Page, ed., *Colonialism: An International Social, Cultural, and Political Encyclopedia* (Santa Barbara, Calif.: ABC-Clio, 2003), 183–85; Peter Lloyd, "The Rise of New Indigenous Elites," in *Colonialism in Africa 1870–1960*, vol. 4: *The Economics of Colonialism*, ed. Peter Duigan and L. H. Gann (Cambridge: Cambridge University Press, 1975), 546–64. See also Wolfgang Mehnert, "Education Policy," in *German Imperialism in Africa*, ed. Helmuth Stoecker (London: C. Hurst, 1986), 216–29.

19. Gerald Meir, "External Trade and Internal Development," in *Colonialism in Africa 1870–1960*, vol. 4: *The Economics of Colonialism*, ed. Peter Duigan and L. H. Gann (Cambridge: Cambridge University Press, 1975), 427–69.

20. Alberto Sbacchi, *Legacy of Bitterness: Ethiopia and Fascist Italy, 1935–1941* (Lawrenceville, N.J.: Red Sea Press, 1997).

21. Fred Lee Hord, *Reconstructing Memory: Black Literary Criticism* (Chicago: Third World Press, 1991).

22. Amilcar Cabral, *Return to the Source* (New York: Africa Information Service, 1973), 39.

23. Bob Blauner, *Still the Big News: Racial Oppression in America* (Philadelphia: Temple University Press, 2001).

24. Homi Bhabha, *The Location of Culture* (London: Routledge, 1994); Stuart Hall, "Cultural Identity and Diaspora," in *Identity: Community, Culture, Difference,* ed. Jonathon Rutherford (London: Lawrence & Wishart, 1990).

25. Homi Bhabha, *Location of Culture.*

26. Blaut, *Colonizer's Model of the World.*

27. See Kirt Wilson, "The Racial Politics of Imitation in the Nineteenth Century," *The Quarterly Journal of Speech* 89.2 (2003): 89–108.

28. John Carlos Rowe, *Literary Culture and U.S. Imperialism* (Oxford: Oxford University Press), 7.

29. Lerone Bennet, *The Shaping of Black America* (Chicago: Johnson, 1975), 208.

30. Blauner, *Still the Big News,* 84.

31. Gilbert Thomas Stephenson, *Race Distinctions in American Law* (New York: AMS Press, 1910).

32. Ronald Buthcart, *Northern Schools, Southern Blacks and Reconstruction: Freedman's Education, 1862–1875* (Westport, Conn.: Greenwood Press, 1980).

33. J. H. O'Dell, "Colonialism and the Negro American Experience," *Freedomways* 6 (1966): 305.

34. William A. Poe, "Lott Cary: Man of Purchased Freedom," *Church History* 39.1 (1970): 49–61.

35. Archibald Alexander, *A History of Colonization on the Western Coast of Africa* (Philadelphia: W. S. Martien, 1846).

36. Lott Cary, cited in John Sailant, "'Circular Addressed to the Colored Brethren and Friends in America': An Unpublished Essay by Lott Cary, sent from Liberia to Virginia, 1827," *The Virginia Magazine of History and Biography* 104.4 (1996): 502.

37. Cary, "Circular," 502.

38. Mary Louise Pratt, "Scratches on the Face of the Country, or What Mr. Barrow Saw in the Land of the Bushmen," in *Race, Writing, and Difference,* ed. Kwame Anthony Appiah and Henry Louis Gates Jr. (Chicago: University of Chicago Press, 1992), 141, 142, 152.

39. Bernard Magubane, *The Ties that Bind: African American Consciousness of Africa* (Trenton, N.J.: Africa World Press, 1987).

40. See Phillip Wander, "Salvation through Separation: The Image of the Negro in the American Colonization Society, *The Quarterly Journal of Speech* 57.1 (1971): 57–67; David M. Streifford, "The American Colonization Society: An Application of Republican Ideology to Early Antebellum Reform" *Journal of Southern History* 45.2 (1979): 201–20.

41. Tom L. Mclaughlin, "Sectional Responses of Free Negroes to the Idea of Colonization," *Research Studies* 34.3 (1996): 126–28.
42. Moses, *Afrotopia.*

2. Black Ethos and the Rhetoric of Pan-Africa

1. For a more thorough history of Black Nationalism, see Rodney P. Carlisle, *The Roots of Black Nationalism* (Port Washington, N.Y.: Kennikat Press, 1975); Michael C. Dawson, *Black Visions: The Roots of Contemporary African-American Political Ideologies* (Chicago: University of Chicago Press, 2001); Essien Udosen Essien-Udom, *Black Nationalism: The Search for an Identity in America* (Chicago: University of Chicago Press, 1969); Dexter B. Gordon, *Black Identity: Rhetoric, Ideology, and Nineteenth-Century Black Nationalism* (Carbondale: Southern Illinois University Press, 2003); Raymond L. Hall, *Black Separatism in the United States* (Hanover, N.H.: University Press of New England, 1978); Augustina Herod and Charles C. Herod, *Afro-American Nationalism: An Annotated Bibliography of Militant Separatist and Nationalist Literature* (New York: Garland, 1986); Wilson Jeremiah Moses, *Classical Black Nationalism: From the American Revolution to Marcus Garvey* (New York: New York University Press, 1996); Jeffrey Ogbonna Green, *Black Power: Radical Politics and African American Identity* (Baltimore: Johns Hopkins University Press, 2004); Alphonso Pinkney, *Red, Black, and Green: Black Nationalism in the United States* (New York: Cambridge University Press, 1978); Dean E. Robinson, *Black Nationalism in American Politics and Thought* (New York: Cambridge University Press, 2001); James Edward Smethurst, *The Black Arts Movement: Literary Nationalism in the 1960s and 1970s* (Chapel Hill: University of North Carolina Press, 2005); Sterling Stuckey, *The Ideological Origins of Black Nationalism* (Boston: Beacon, 1972). For more thorough discussion of the image of Africa in black American public discourse, see Adelaide Cromwell and Martin Kilson, *Apropos of Africa: Sentiments of Negro American Leaders on Africa from the 1800s to the 1950s* (London: Frank Cass, 1969); E. U. Essien-Udom, "Black Identity in the International Context," in *Key Issues in the Afro-American Experience,* vol. 2: *Since 1865,* ed. Nathan Huggins, Martin Kilson, and Daniel Fox (New York: Harcourt Brace Jovanovich, 1971); E. U. Essien-Udom, "The Relationship of Afro-Americans to African Nationalism," *Freedomways* 2 (1962): 391–407; Harold Isaacs, "The American Negro and Africa: Some Notes," *Phylon* 20 (1959): 219–33; Richard B. Moore, "Africa Conscious Harlem," *Freedomways* 3 (1963): 315–34; George Shepperson, "Notes on Negro American Influence on the Emergence of African Nationalism," *Journal of African History* 1.2 (1960): 299–312.
2. Tunde Adeleke, *UnAfrican Americans: Nineteenth-Century Black Nationalists and the Civilizing Mission* (Lexington: University Press of Kentucky, 1998).
3. Joseph E. Holloway, ed., *Africanisms in American Culture* (Bloomington: Indiana University Press, 1990).

4. Celeste Condit and John Lucaites, *Crafting Equality: America's Anglo-African Word* (Chicago: University of Chicago Press, 1993).

5. Benedict Anderson argues for a coincidence between the modern nation, colonial ideology, and imperialist practices. In this case, as black Americans imagined black ethos during this period, they participated in and contributed to this emerging rhetoric of nationhood. See Benedict Anderson, *Imagined Communities: Reflections on the Origin and Spread of Nationalism* (London: Verso, 1983).

6. Michael Hyde, "Introduction: Rhetorically We Dwell," in *The Ethos of Rhetoric*, ed. Michael Hyde (Columbia: University of South Carolina Press, 2004), xiii.

7. The internalization of pathological senses of "blackness" is well studied; W. E. B. Du Bois and Frantz Fanon, for example, both discuss how individuals in the African Diaspora come to know themselves through the semiotic frames of white supremacy. See W. E. B. Du Bois, *The Souls of Black Folk* (New York: Viking Penguin, 1996); Frantz Fanon, *Black Skin, White Masks* (New York: Grove, 1967).

8. Eric King Watts, "The Ethos of a Black Aesthetic: An Exploration of Larry Neal's Visions of a Liberated Future," in *The Ethos of Rhetoric*, ed. Michael Hyde (Columbia: University of South Carolina Press, 2004), 98–113.

9. Imanuel Geiss, *The Pan-African Movement* (London: Methuen, 1974), 4.

10. Charles Andrain defines Pan-Africanism as "an inclusive movement seeking to realize the unity transcending the European made boundaries now dividing the African continent"(6). Keiko Kusunose argues that Pan-Africanism is "the manifestation of a social movement of international solidarity among people who have made a contribution to the promotion of the cause of African people and people of African descent all over the world" (45). George Padmore claims that "the idea of Pan Africanism first arose as a manifestation of fraternal solidarity among Africans and peoples of African descent" (95). Robert Chrisman suggests that the "Pan African vision has as its basic premise that we the people of African descent throughout the globe constitute a common cultural and political community by virtue of our origin in Africa and our common racial, social and economic oppression"(2). John Henrik Clarke claims that Pan-Africanism is "about the restoration of African people to their proper place in world history" (99). Kwadwo Osei-Nyame claims that "Pan-Africanism can in a general conceptual sense be said to encompass all the discourses, ideologies and cultural and political practices which have to date been mobilized as a means of confronting the historical derogation and subjugation of African peoples"(137). Tamba M'bayo defines Pan-Africanism as the "perceived need to mobilize all peoples of African descent against racism and colonialism"(21). Perhaps one of the most comprehensive and useful definitions of Pan-Africanism is Peter O. Esedebe's claim that Pan-Africanism has seven main components: "Africa as the homeland of Africans and persons of African origin, solidarity among people of African descent, belief in a distinct African personality, rehabilitation of Africa's past, pride in African culture, Africa for Africans in church and state, and the hope for a united and glorious future Africa"(4). See Charles Andrauin, "The Pan-African Movement: The Search for Organization and Community," *Phylon* 1 (1962): 5–17; Robert

Chrisman and Nathan Hare, *Pan-Africanism* (Indianapolis: Bobbs-Merrill, 1974); John Henrik Clarke, "Pan-Africanism: A Brief History of an Idea in the African World," *Third World First* 1.2 (1990): 9–28; Peter Olisanwuche Esedebe, *Pan-Africanism: The Idea and Movement, 1776–1991* (Washington, D.C.: Howard University, 1994). Tamba E. M'bayo, "W. E. B. Du Bois, Marcus Garvey, and Pan-Africanism in Liberia, 1919–1924," *Historian* 66.1 (2004): 19–44; Isidore Okpewho, Carole Boyce Davies, and Ali Al Amin Mazrui, *The African Diaspora: African Origins and New World Identities* (Bloomington: Indiana University Press, 1999); Kwadwo Osei-Nyame, "Pan-Africanist Ideology and the African Historical Novel of Self-Discovery: The Examples of Kobina Sekyi and J. E. Casely Hayford," *Journal of African Cultural Studies* 12.2 (1999): 137–53. For further information about Pan-Africanism generally, see Adekunle Ajala, *Pan-Africanism: Evolution, Progress, and Prospects* (New York: St. Martin's, 1973); S. K. B. Asante, *Pan-African Protest: West Africa and the Italo-Ethiopian Crisis, 1934–1941* (London: Longman, 1977); St. Clair Drake, "The Black Diaspora in Pan-African Perspective," *Black Scholar* 7.1 (1975): 2–13; Milfred C. Fierce, *The Pan-African Idea in the United States, 1900–1919: African-American Interest in Africa and Interaction with West Africa* (New York: Garland, 1993); Robert A. Hill, *Pan-African Biography* (Los Angeles, Calif.: African Studies Center University of California Los Angeles and Crossroads Press / African Studies Association, 1987); Michael W. Williams, *Pan-Africanism: An Annotated Bibliography* (Pasadena, Calif.: Salem Press, 1993).

11. Drake's interpretation of black American political and cultural investment in Africa is one of the most complete narratives of the relationship between black America and Africa. See St. Clair Drake, "Negro Americans and the Africa Interest," in *The American Negro Reference Book,* ed. John P. Davis (Englewood Cliffs, N.J.: Prentice Hall, 1966), 662–705. Perhaps the clearest articulation of the theoretical understanding of diaspora can be found in James Clifford, "Diasporas," *Cultural Anthropology* 9.3 (1994): 302–38. Brent Hayes Edwards traces the academic use of the term "diaspora" in "The Uses of Diaspora," *Social Text* 19.1 (2001): 45–73.

12. George Shepperson, "Pan-Africanism and 'pan-Africanism': Some Historical Notes," *Phylon* 4.4 (1962): 346–58.

13. Ibid., 346.

14. Wilson Jeremiah Moses, for example, implicitly defines Pan-Africanism by contrasting Pan-African activity with Black Nationalist thought. Moses argues that although both terms describe visions of empowered black identity, Black Nationalists employ that vision in the quest for a separate black state. Thus, in Moses's calculus, Pan-Africanism is ambiguously related to political power. It is a cultural movement, whereas Black Nationalism is a political one. See Wilson Jeremiah Moses, *Classical Black Nationalism: From the American Revolution to Marcus Garvey.*

15. Michael W. Williams, "Pan-Africanism and Zionism: The Delusion of Comparability," *Journal of Black Studies* 21.3 (1991): 348–71.

16. Kwame Nantambu, "Pan-Africanism versus Pan-African Nationalism: An Afrocentric Analysis," *Journal of Black Studies* 28.5 (1998): 561–74.

17. Sidney J. Lemelle and Robin D. G. Kelley, "Introduction: Imagining Home: Pan-Africanism Revisited," in *Imagining Home: Class, Culture, and Nationalism in the African Diaspora,* ed. Sidney J. Lemelle and Robin D. G. Kelley (London: Verso, 1994), 1–16.

18. Sidney J. Lemelle, "The Politics of Cultural Existence: Pan-Africanism, Historical Materialism, and Afrocentricity," in *Imagining Home: Class, Culture, and Nationalism in the African Diaspora,* ed. Sidney J. Lemelle and Robin D. G. Kelley (London: Verso, 1994), 331–50.

19. Robert Terrill and Eric King Watts, "W. E. B. Du Bois, Double Consciousness, and Pan-Africanism in the Progressive Era," in *Rhetoric and Reform in the Progressive Era,* ed. J. M. Hogan (East Lansing: Michigan State University Press, 2002), 269–309.

20. Lucy Craft Laney, Mary Church Terrell, and Victoria Earle Mathews, for example, lobbied for racial uplift through a reconfiguration of the private sphere. They argued that proliferation and refinement of middle-class habits in African American families would combat race prejudice and lead to political and economic progress. See Lucy Craft Laney, "The Burden of the Educated Colored Woman," in *Lift Every Voice: African American Oratory, 1787–1900,* ed. Phillip Sheldon Foner and Robert James Branham (Tuscaloosa: University of Alabama Press, 1998).

21. Kevin Gaines illustrates relationships among the ideology of uplift, imperial discourse, and characterizations of Africa. See Kevin Gaines, *Uplifting the Race: Black Leadership, Politics, and Culture in the Twentieth Century* (Chapel Hill: University of North Carolina Press, 1996).

22. Cheryl Lynn Greenberg, *Or Does It Explode? Black Harlem in the Great Depression* (New York: Oxford University Press, 1991). Wilson Jeremiah Moses, "The Lost World of the Negro, 1895–1919: Black Literary and Intellectual Life before the 'Renaissance,'" *Black American Literature Forum* 21.1/2 (1987): 61–84.

23. Marc Gallicchio, *The African American Encounter with Japan and China: Black Internationalism in Asia, 1895–1945* (Chapel Hill: University of North Carolina Press, 2000).

24. See Wilson Jeremiah Moses, "Civilizing Missionary: A Study of Alexander Crummell," *Journal of Negro History* 60.2 (1975): 229–51.

25. Terril and Watts trace the development of "Africa interest" in Du Bois's editorials in *The Horizon* and *The Crisis.* See Terrill and Watts, "W. E. B. Du Bois, Double Consciousness and Pan-Africanism in the Progressive Era."

26. W. E. B. Du Bois, *Darkwater: Voices from within the Veil* ([1920]; New York: Dover, 1999), 32.

27. Ibid., 36.

28. W. E. B. Du Bois and Augustus Dill, *Morals and Manners among Negro Americans* (Atlanta: Atlanta University, 1914), 67. Other black Americans made similar arguments. In a 1918 pamphlet, *Children of the Sun,* George Wells Parker

reminisced about the time when "our dusky mother held the stage . . . and gave birth to nations." Cited in Moses, *Afrotopia*, 89.

29. See Alexander Goldenweiser, "Diffusionism and the American School of Historical Ethnology," *The American Journal of Sociology* 31.1 (1925): 19–38. Franz Boas also used the theory of diffusionism to argue against a single, normative evolutionary pattern for cultural development. For Boas, diffusion explained the growth of folk cultures in the interstices between cultures. See Franz Boas, "Evolution or Diffusion," *American Anthropologist* 26.3 (1924): 340–44. For other examples of the debate over diffusionism leading up to the 1930s, see John Owen Clark, "Diffusion Center vs. Melting Pot," *American Anthropologist* 29.4 (1927): 732–33; T. F. Crane, "The Diffusion of Popular Tales," *Journal of American Folklore* 1.1 (1888): 8–15; Harold S. Gladwin, "Independent Invention versus Diffusion," *American Antiquity* 3.2 (1937): 156–60; A. L. Kroeber, "Stimulus Diffusion," *American Anthropologist* 42.1 (1940): 1–20; R. R. Marett, *The Diffusion of Culture* (Cambridge: Cambridge University Press, 1927); W. W. Newell, "Theories of Diffusion of Folk-Tales," *Journal of American Folklore* 8.28 (1895): 7–18; Grafton Elliot Smith et al., *Culture, the Diffusion Controversy* (New York: W. W. Norton, 1927); Julian H. Steward, "Diffusion and Independent Invention: A Critique of Logic," *American Anthropologist* 31.3 (1929): 491–95; Wilson D. Wallis, "Probability and the Diffusion of Culture Traits," *American Anthropologist* 30.1 (1928): 94–106.

30. Eric King Watts, "Pragmatist Publicity: W. E. B. Du Bois and the New Negro Movement," in *Public Modalities: Rhetoric, Culture, Media, and the Shape of Public Life*, ed. Daniel C. Brouer and Robert Asen (Tuscaloosa: University of Alabama Press, 2010), 33–59.

31. Moses, *Afrotopia*.

32. Du Bois, *Darkwater*, 35.

33. Ibid., 37.

34. Ibid., 40.

35. W. E. B. Du Bois, "The Future of Africa," *Advocate of Peace* 81 (1919): 12–13.

36. Du Bois was not the first person to suggest that black people share a culture irrespective of the state in which they reside, but his vision of Pan-African community was particularly impactful in that it helped establish an international frame for subsequent conversations about black identity.

37. W. E. B. Du Bois, "The Conservation of Races," *The Conservation of Races and the Negro* (Washington, D.C.: The American Negro Academy Occasional Papers, 1897), 5–18. Earlwright2.com (accessed Sept. 21, 2011).

38. Moses, *Afrotopia*.

39. Terrill and Watts, "W. E. B. Du Bois, Double Consciousness, and Pan-Africanism in the Progressive Era."

40. See Judith Stein, *The World of Marcus Garvey: Race and Class in Modern Society* (Baton Rouge: Louisiana State University Press, 1986).

41. Greenberg, *Or Does It Explode?*

42. See Robert E. Park, "The Concept of Social Distance," *Journal of Applied Sociology* 8 (1924): 339–44. For further discussion of Park's racial philosophy, see

R. Fred Wacker, *Race and Ethnicity in American Social Science, 1900–1950* (Ann Arbor: University of Michigan Press, 1975).

43. Cited in Colin Grant, *Negro with a Hat: The Rise and Fall of Marcus Garvey* (Oxford: Oxford University Press, 2008), 52.

44. Marcus Garvey, "African Fundamentalism," in *Marcus Garvey and the Vision of Africa,* ed. John Henrick Clarke (New York: Vintage Books, 1974), 156.

45. Ibid., 157.

46. Ibid.

47. Marcus Garvey, "Untitled Speech at Liberty Hall," in *The Marcus Garvey and Universal Negro Improvement Association Papers,* ed. Robert A. Hill (Berkeley: University of California Press, 1983), 503.

48. Marcus Garvey, "Africa for the Africans," in *Philosophy and Opinions of Marcus Garvey,* ed. Amy Jacques Garvey (New York: Atheneum, 1971), 68.

49. Cited in Grant, *Negro with a Hat,* 44.

50. Garvey, "Africa for the Africans," 70.

51. Constitution of the U.N.I.A., cited in James A. Meriwether, *Proudly We Can Be Africans: Black Americans and Africa, 1935–1961* (Chapel Hill: University of North Carolina Press, 2002), 22.

52. Garvey, "African Fundamentalism," 159.

53. Kenneth Burke, *A Grammar of Motives* (Berkeley: University of California Press, 1945), 507.

54. See Hollis Lynch, ed., *Black Spokesman: Selected Writings of Edward Wilmot Blyden* (New York: Humanities Press, 1971). For Crummell's attitude toward African community, see Alexander Crummel, "The Destined Superiority of the Negro," in *Destiny and Race: Selected Writings, 1840–1898,* ed. Wilson Jeremiah Moses (Amherst: University of Massachusetts Press, 1992): 194–205.

55. Chantal Mouffe, "Toward a Radical Democratic Citizenship," *Democratic Left* 17.2 (1989): 7.

56. As is evident in the history described in this essay, many black American individuals had political and economic relationships with people throughout the African Diaspora. However, another benefit of Schmitt's terminology is that he discusses public expressions of community and brackets out interpersonal relations as a distinct phenomenon.

57. "Two Dead, Many Hurt in Chicago Riot," the *New York Times,* June 21, 1920.

58. Moses, *Afrotopia,* 40.

3. *"Unhappy Haiti"*

1. "To Americans, Dessalines was the sinister figure representing a long line of violent, vengeful rulers; Toussaint represented stability and forgiveness"; Alfred N. Hunt, *Haiti's Influence on Antebellum America: Slumbering Volcano in the Caribbean* (Baton Rouge: Louisiana State University Press, 1988), 91.

2. Brenda Gayle Plummer, "The Afro-American Response to the Occupation of Haiti, 1915–1934," *Phylon* 43.2 (1982): 127.

3. Some black Americans did address U.S. imperialism in the Pacific, but these foreign policy actions were not discussed with anything like the intensity or frequency of U.S. policy in Haiti. See Marc Gallicchio, *The African American Encounter with Japan and China: Black Internationalism in Asia, 1895–1945* (Chapel Hill: University of North Carolina Press, 2000).

4. Woodrow Wilson, "Speech at the Southern Commercial Congress," in *The Papers of Woodrow Wilson,* ed. Arthur S. Link (Princeton, N.J.: Princeton University Press, 1966), 448–53.

5. Wilson's assumption was not completely without justification. Both established governments and insurgent groups were engaged with U.S. and European banks.

6. See Brenda Gayle Plummer, *Haiti and the United States: The Psychological Moment* (Athens: University of Georgia Press, 1992); Hans Schmidt, *The United States Occupation of Haiti, 1915–1934* (New Brunswick, N.J.: Rutgers University Press, 1971).

7. See Mary Renda, *Taking Haiti: Military Occupation and the Culture of U.S. Imperialism, 1915–1940* (Chapel Hill: University of North Carolina Press, 2001).

8. Walker, cited in Plummer, *Haiti and the United States,* 108.

9. Rayford Logan, *Haiti and the Dominican Republic* (London: Oxford University Press, 1968), 126.

10. Baringer, cited in Panphile, *Haitians and African Americans,* 106.

11. Plummer, *Haiti and the United States.*

12. Booker T. Washington, "Haiti and the United States," *Outlook,* November 17, 1915, 105.

13. Henry Louis Suggs, "The Response of the African-American Press to the United States Occupation of Haiti, 1915–1934," *Journal of Negro History* 73.1 (2002): 35.

14. Ibid.

15. *Negro World,* February 26, 1931.

16. Perceval Thoby and Steinio Vincent, "Latin America Desires Self-Government," *Negro World,* 1921, sec. Letters.

17. James Weldon Johnson, "Government of, by, and for the National City Bank," *The Nation* 111 (1920): 297.

18. James Weldon Johnson, "The Truth about Haiti," *The Crisis* 20 (1920): 218.

19. Cited in Robert Milde, "The Harp and the Sword: Rhetorical Depictions of Haiti in Early Twentieth Century United States Literature," (PhD diss., University of North Carolina at Greensboro, 1999), 251.

20. James Weldon Johnson, "What the United States Has Accomplished," *The Nation* 111 (1920): 265.

21. Pamphile, *Haitians and African Americans;* Plummer, *Haiti and the United States.*

22. See Brenda Gayle Plummer, "The Afro-American Response."

23. See John Blassingame, "The Press and American Intervention in Haiti and the Dominican Republic, 1904–1920," *Caribbean Studies* (1969): 27–43.

24. Plummer, "The Afro-American Response."

25. Oscar De Priest, "Speech," *The Congressional Record,* December 18, 1929, 913.

26. "U.S. Marine Rule in Haiti Seen as Colossal Failure." *New York Amsterdam News* December 11 1929, 1.

27. Though essentially representative of and read by the black middle class, black periodicals were sources of information about the events in Africa and the African Diaspora from a friendly source, one that could be trusted to demonstrate a black perspective. In the nineteenth century, most black newspapers were beholden to patronage or political sponsorship, as were many European American periodicals. Editorial power resided in a few individuals like Booker T. Washington, who wielded considerable power over many aspects of black public life at the turn of the century. From 1900 to 1930 the number of black periodicals grew to 1,400, but still, black newspapers struggled commercially. The *Chicago Defender* was one of the first successful black periodicals that could survive on profit from its circulation and advertising. Founded in 1905, the *Defender* adopted the sensationalistic techniques of William Randolph Hearst to develop a mass readership. The *Pittsburgh Courier,* however, achieved some success with a more political reputation. The circulation of most black periodicals peaked in 1919. Even *The Crisis,* one of the few black periodicals that had the support of organizational capital and distribution and a biracial readership, experienced a marked decline in circulation after 1919, plummeting from an average circulation of 94,408 in 1919 to around 30,000 in 1930. I focus on the *Chicago Defender, Pittsburgh Courier,* and *New York Amsterdam News* because they were the major national papers in black America during the Great Depression. See Michael Fultz, "'The Morning Cometh': African-American Periodicals, Education, and the Black Middle Class, 1900–1930," *Journal of Negro History* (1995): 97–112; T. Ella Strother, "The Race-Advocacy Function of the Black Press," *Black American Literature Forum* (1978): 92–99.

28. "In Troubled Haiti," *Chicago Defender,* December 28, 1929, Other Papers Say sec., 12.

29. "Cossacks in Haiti," *New York Amsterdam News,* December 11, 1929, Editorial sec., 30.

30. "A Black Dictator," *Pittsburgh Courier,* October 26, 1929, Editorial sec.

31. Harry Johnson, "Haiti and Its Regeneration by the United States," *The National Geographic Magazine,* December 1920, 497–505. Indeed, one picture published in this article literally depicted the business of the Haitian government proceeding under the watchful eye of a U.S. Marine. This picture infuriated progressive Americans, who saw it as evidence of the real motivation behind the occupation.

32. *Chicago Defender,* December 7, 1929, Front Page sec., 1.

33. "Borah and Haiti," *New York Amsterdam News,* January 8, 1930, Editorial sec.

34. "Cossacks in Haiti," *New York Amsterdam News,* December 11, 1929, Editorial sec., 30.

35. Joel A. Rogers, "Will We Get out of Haiti," *New York Amsterdam News,* February 5, 1930, Editorial sec.

36. "The Haitian Commission," *New York Amsterdam News,* March 12, 1930, Editorial sec.

37. "Cossacks in Haiti."

38. "Conditions in Haiti," *Chicago Defender,* December 21, 1929, Editorial sec., 17.

39. "Appoint a Negro," *New York Amsterdam News,* December 18, 1929, Editorial sec.

40. Kelly Miller, "The Haitian Commission," *New York Amsterdam News,* February 5, 1930, Editorial sec.

41. Dantes Belegrande, "The American Occupation of Haiti: Its Moral and Economic Effects," *Opportunity,* January 1930, 10.

42. "Trouble in Haiti," *Chicago Defender,* December 14, 1929, Editorial sec.

43. In 1849 Douglass wrote that it was "idle — worse than idle, ever to think of our expatriation or removal." Later, in his celebrated "The Meaning of July Fourth for the Negro" address, Douglass argued that individuals who agitated for black civil rights were the true inheritors of the spirit of the American Revolution. Throughout his public career, Douglass fought to achieve American citizenship rights for black Americans. See Frederick Douglass, "The Destiny of Colored Americans," *The North Star,* November 16, 1849; Frederick Douglass, "The Meaning of July Fourth for the Negro," in *Frederick Douglas: Selected Speeches and Writings,* ed. Phillip Foner (Chicago: Lawrence Hill Books, 2000), 188–206.

44. Early in 1930, the Hoover administration gave in to pressure from the president of Haiti and domestic political groups by declining to appoint a U.S. black American to the committee. Instead, he appointed a secondary commission to report on the Haitian educational system. African American Robert Russa Moton, inheritor of Booker T. Washington's ethos and authority at Tuskeegee, headed this subordinate commission.

45. Kelly Miller, "The Haitian Commission."

46. Prominent U.S. black Americans John Mercer Langston and Frederick Douglass served subsequently. Although the position held great prestige for African Americans, Douglass's tenure ended unsatisfactorily. His frustrated efforts to achieve a refueling station for U.S. marines at the Haitian port of Mole St. Michel reminded black Americans of Douglass's earlier sympathy for U.S. annexation of the Dominican Republic in 1871. His service as minister to Haiti was widely criticized and figured in arguments about his loyalty to "the" race.

47. Suggs, "The Response of the African American Press."

48. Michael Krenn, *Black Diplomacy: African Americans and the State Department, 1945–1969* (Armonk, N.Y.: M. E. Sharpe, 1999).

49. Kelly Miller, "The Haitian Commission."

50. George Little, "Haiti and the White Press," *Chicago Defender,* December 28, 1929, Letters sec., 12.

51. Ibid.

52. Ibid.

53. W. E. B. Du Bois, cited in *The Correspondence of W. E. B. Du Bois,* Vol. 1: *1877–1934,* ed. Herbert Apthecker (Boston: University of Massachusetts Press, 1973), 212.

54. Ibid.

55. "Our Policy on Haiti Scored in Debate," *New York Times,* December 22, 1929.

56. Plummer, *Haiti and the United States.*
57. Quoted in Robert A. Hill, "Introduction," *Ethiopian Stories* (Boston: Northeastern University Press, 1994).

4. "Modern" Slaves

1. I. K. Sundiata, *Black Scandal: America and the Liberian Labor Crisis* (Philadelphia: Institute for the Study of Human Issues, 1980), 84–85.
2. George S. Schuyler, *Black and Conservative: The Autobiography of George Samuel Schuyler* (New Rochelle, N.Y.: Arlington House, 1966); George S. Schuyler, "The Negro Art Hokum," *The Nation,* no. 122, June 16, 1926, 662–63.
3. In one of those essays, Schuyler suggested a plan to liberate indigenous Liberians from the oppression of the Americo-Liberian oligarchy. He mused that it was "high time" for "an expeditionary force of about 500 Aframericans, liberally supplied with rifles, machine guns, and ammunition to set sail for the West African republic." These articles caused considerable consternation: Liberian president Edwin Barclay and NAACP president Walter White both attacked Schuyler in print, impugning both his journalistic integrity for his publication of "legends" and his racial consciousness for censuring Liberia while even white missionaries came to its "defense." And yet Schuyler's articles clearly demonstrated a frame in which the "real" politics and culture of indigenous Africa resonated with African America. See Robert A. Hill, "Introduction," *Ethiopian Stories* (Boston: Northeastern University Press, 1994).
4. Michael W. Peplow, *George S. Schuyler* (Boston: Twayne, 1980), 99.
5. Most criticism of Schuyler's work focuses on his personal politics. See Henry Louis Gates Jr., "A Fragmented Man: George Schuyler and the Claims of Race," *New York Times,* September 20, 1992; Ann Rayson, "George Schuyler: Paradox among 'Assimilationist' Writers," *Black American Literature Forum* 12 (1978): 102–6; Stacy Morgan, "'The Strange and Wonderful Workings of Science': Race Science and Essentialism in George Schuyler's *Black No More*," *College Language Association Journal* 3 (1999): 331–52; Jeffery A. Tucker, "'Can Science Succeed Where the Civil War Failed?' George Schuyler and Race," in *Race-Consciousness: African-American Studies for a New Century,* ed. Judith Jackson Fossett and Jeffery A. Tucker (New York: New York University Press, 1997), 136–53; James O. Young, *Black Writers of the Thirties* (Baton Rouge: Louisiana State University Press, 1973).
6. J. Gus Liebnow, *Liberia: The Quest for Democracy* (Bloomington: Indiana University Press, 1987). This social stratification resulted in a number of violent conflicts between Americo-Liberians and indigenous Liberian tribes. The intensity and frequency of these conflicts increased dramatically between 1910 and 1920. See Jo Sullivan, "The Kru Coast Revolt of 1915–1916," *Liberian Studies Journal* 14 (1989): 51–71.
7. Sundiata, *Black Scandal,* 24–25.
8. Raymond L. Buell, cited in Sundiata, *Black Scandal,* 172.

9. Sundiata, *Black Scandal,* 141, 1–2.

10. See Arthur Knoll, "Harvey Firestone's Liberian Investment (1922–1932)," *Liberian Studies Journal* 14 (1989): 13–33; Alfred Lief, *The Firestone Story: A History of the Firestone Rubber Company* (New York: Whittlesey House, 1951).

11. "Liberian Freedmen Hold Slaves," *New York Amsterdam News,* October 22, 1930, 1.

12. W. E. B. Du Bois, "Liberia, the League, and the United States," *Foreign Affairs* 11.4 (1933): 682–95; W. E. B. Du Bois, "Post Script — Liberia," *The Crisis,* March 1931, 102.

13. Du Bois, "Post Script — Liberia," 102.

14. Johnson, "Liberia," *The Crisis,* April 1931, 172.

15. Alain Locke made a similar argument about the essentially "modern" nature of the Liberian crisis. According to him, the modern condition made new insidious oppressions possible. See Alain Locke, "Slavery in the Modern Manner," *Survey,* March 31, 1931, 591.

16. Nnandi Azikiwe, "In Defense of Liberia," *Journal of Negro History* 17.1 (1932): 30–50.

17. Edwin Barclay, "The Case of Liberia," *The Crisis,* February 1934, 40–42.

18. Peplow, *George S. Schuyler.*

19. George Schuyler, *Slaves Today: A Story of Liberia* (New York: Brewer Warren & Putnam, 1931), 6.

20. Peplow, *George S. Schuyler.*

21. Schuyler, *Slaves Today,* 36–37.

22. John Cullen Gruesser, *Black on Black: Twentieth-Century African American Writing about Africa* (Lexington: University Press of Kentucky, 2000).

23. Schuyler, *Slaves Today,* 23, 12–13.

24. Alain Locke, "The Legacy of the Ancestral Arts," in *The New Negro,* ed. Alain Locke (New York: Simon & Schuster, 1925).

25. "Schuyler Defends Liberian Expose," *New York Amsterdam News,* August 12, 1931, 1–2.

26. For example, in his 1936 science-fiction serial set in Africa and published in the *Pittsburgh Courier,* "The Black Internationale: A Story of Black Genius against the World," Schuyler's "Genius," Dr. Belsidus, builds a Pan-African community through overtly manipulative religious ceremonies designed to perpetuate an Afro-Diasporic community. See George S. Schuyler, *Black Empire* (Boston: Northeastern University Press, 1991).

27. "Schuyler Defends Liberian Exposé," *New York Amsterdam News.*

28. Schuyler, *Slaves Today,* 116.

29. Rudolph Fisher, "City of Refuge," in *The New Negro,* ed. Alain Locke (New York: Simon & Schuster, 1925), 57–58.

30. Henry Louis Gates Jr., "Of Negroes Old and New," *Transition* (1974): 44–58; Houston A. Baker Jr., *Modernism and the Harlem Renaissance* (Chicago: University of Chicago Press, 1987).

31. Robert A. Hill, "Introduction," *Ethiopian Stories* (Boston: Northeastern University Press, 1994).

32. Eugène Sue, *Les Mystères de Paris* (Paris: Pauvert, 1963).

33. Umberto Eco, "Rhetoric and Ideology in Eugène Sue's Les Mystères de Paris," *International Social Science Journal* 19.4 (1967): 555–71.

34. Ronald J. Zboray and Mary Saracino Zboray, "The Mysteries of New England: Eugène Sue's American 'Imitators,' 1844," *Nineteenth Century Concepts* 22 (2000): 457–92.

35. Richard Slotkin, *Gunfighter Nation: The Myth of the Frontier in Twentieth-Century America* (Norman: Oklahoma University Press) 194.

36. Marianna Torgovnick, *Gone Primitive: Savage Intellects, Modern Lives* (Chicago: University of Chicago Press, 1990).

37. Ishmael Reed, *Mumbo Jumbo* (Garden City, N.Y.: Doubleday, 1972).

38. Slotkin, *Gunfighter Nation,* 222.

39. Rudolph Fisher, *The Conjure-Man Dies: A Mystery Tale of Dark Harlem 1932* (Ann Arbor: University of Michigan Press, 1992); George S. Schuyler, *Black No More* (College Park, Md.: McGrath, 1969).

40. Schuyler's later novellas, serialized in the *Pittsburgh Courier* and set in both Africa and Harlem, used the detective prototype explicitly. In "An Ethiopian Murder Mystery," Schuyler's artistic response to the Italian invasion of Ethiopia, the protagonist, Rod, solves the murder of a visiting Ethiopian prince. Rod's independent, intuitive sleuthing makes a mockery of the pretensions, sloth, and myopia of the official detective assigned to the case. Schuyler's own journalistic practices exemplified this model as well.

41. Schuyler, *Slaves Today,* 155, 173, 179.

42. Citing his science-fiction fantasies like the "Black Internationale" series, Fritz Gysin argues that Schuyler's fiction is merely a repetition of the discourses of American imperialism. According to Gysin, Schuyler's distinctly American protagonists are part of a colonial project. However, Gysin neglects the larger context of black anticolonialism and Schuyler's own evolving understanding of the African Diaspora. See Fritz Gysin, "Black Pulp Fiction: George Schuyler's Caustic Vision of a Panafrican Empire," in *Empire: American Studies,* ed. John G. Blair and Reinhold Wagnleitner (Tübingen: Selected Papers from the Bi-National Conference of the Swiss and Austrian Associations for American Studies at the Salzburg Seminar, 1996), 167–79.

43. W. E. B. Du Bois, *The Souls of Black Folk* (New York: Viking Penguin, 1996).

44. W. E. B. Du Bois, "The Souls of White Folk," in *Darkwater: Voices from within the Veil* (New York: Dover, 1999), 17–29.

45. Harvard Sitkoff, *A New Deal for Blacks: The Emergence of Civil Rights as a National Issue* (Oxford: Oxford University Press, 1978).

46. Sundiata, *Black Scandal.*

47. Johnson, cited in Sundiata, *Black Scandal,* 85.

48. Cited in Frank Chalk, "The Anatomy of Investment: Firestone's 1927 Loan to Liberia," *Canadian Journal of African Studies* 1.1 (1967): 24.

49. Houston A. Baker Jr. *Turning South Again: Re-Thinking Modernism / Re-Reading Booker T.* (Durham, N.C.: Duke University Press, 2001).

50. Robin D. G. Kelley, *Race Rebels: Culture, Politics and the Black Working Class* (New York: The Free Press, 1994).

51. Padmore left the party in 1933 and wrote a number of essays that critiqued the CPUSA for its opportunism and absence of a genuine interest in the health of black America. Padmore's decision was inspired by Russia's capitulation to European imperialism and the ILD's (the legal wing of the CPUSA) handling of the Scottsboro and Angelo Herndon cases. See Hakim Adi and Marika Sherwood, *Pan-African History: Political Figures from Africa and the Diaspora since 1787* (London: Routledge, 2003); James R. Hooker, *Black Revolutionary: George Padmore's Path from Communism to Pan-Africanism* (New York: Praeger, 1970).

52. Schuyler, *Black and Conservative,* 240.

53. Michael Denning, *The Cultural Front: The Laboring of American Culture in the Twentieth Century* (New York: Verso, 1996).

54. Jon Woodson, *To Make a New Race: Gurdjieff, Toomer, and the Harlem Renaissance* (Jackson: University Press of Mississippi, 1999).

55. Sitkoff, *A New Deal for Blacks.*

56. W. E. B. Du Bois, "The Browsing Reader," *The Crisis* (February 1932): 68.

57. Du Bois, "The Browsing Reader."

5. Ethiopia Is Now

1. George Shepperson, "Ethiopianism and African Nationalism," *Phylon* (1953): 9–18; Robert G. Weisbord, *Ebony Kinship: Africa, Africans, and the Afro-American* (Westport, Conn.: Greenwood Press, 1973).

2. St. Clair Drake has identified four central tenets of Ethiopianist thought. First, Ethiopianism assumes a common ancestry that linked African Americans and the African Diaspora. Second, it implies a cyclical view of history in which cultures suffered periods of decline but also could anticipate eventual redemption. Third, it posits that Africa owned a glorious past. And fourth, Ethiopianism predicts a future in which Africa would be redeemed because of European, Christian civilization and power. In this final, prophetic dimension, Ethiopianism forecast the coming of a renewed African race freed from both exploitation and paganism. See St. Clair Drake, *The Redemption of Africa and Black Religion* (Chicago: Third World, 1970).

3. Joseph E. Harris, *African-American Reactions to War in Ethiopia, 1936–1941* (Baton Rouge: Louisiana State University Press, 1994).

4. Father Divine's Peace Mission was a biracial organization that inherited much of Garvey's popularity in the 1930s. Father Divine incorporated Eastern mysticism, a communitarian imperative, and progressive antiracialist beliefs in a far-reaching social program. See Jill Watts, *God, Harlem, U.S.A.: The Father Divine Story* (Berkeley: University of California Press, 1992).

5. Though a minority voice, several black Americans solicited volunteers to go to Ethiopia and fight on its behalf. From 1935 to early 1936 Sufi Abdul Hamid (the "Black Hitler of Harlem," who would later appear, fictionalized, in Ishmael Reed's

Mumbo Jumbo) and Samuel Daniels of the Pan-African Reconstruction Association organized volunteers to fight in Ethiopia until the U.S. State department declared that fighting for a foreign government would jeopardize one's U.S. citizenship (despite eventual mayor La Guardia's tenure in the Italian army fifteen years earlier). See Ishmael Reed, *Mumbo Jumbo* (Garden City, N.Y.: Doubleday, 1972); William R. Scott, *The Son's of Sheba's Race: African-Americans and the Italo-Ethiopian War, 1935–1941* (Bloomington: Indiana University Press, 1993).

6. Roi Ottley, *"New World a-Coming": Inside Black America* (Boston: Houghton Mifflin, 1943), 104.

7. John Hope Franklin, *From Slavery to Freedom: A History of Negro Americans* (New York: Knopf, 1967), 385.

8. See Firku Gebrekidan, "In Defense of Ethiopia: A Comparative Assessment of Caribbean and African-American Anti-Fascist Protests, 1935–1941," *Northeast African Studies* 2.1 (1995): 145–73; Joseph E. Harris, *African-American Reactions to War in Ethiopia, 1936–1941* (Baton Rouge: Louisiana State University Press, 1994); Dennis C. Hickey, "Positive Perspectives on Independent Africa: Ethiopia, Liberia, and the American Popular Press, 1920–1935," *Africana Journal* 17 (1998): 257–70; Bernard Magubane, *The Ties That Bind: African-American Consciousness of Africa* (Trenton, N.J.: Africa World Press, 1987); Scott, *The Sons of Sheba's Race;* William A. Shack, "Ethiopia and Afro Americans: Some Historical Notes, 1920–1970," *Phylon* 35 (1974): 142–55; Robert G. Weisbord, *Ebony Kinship: Africa, Africans, and the Afro-American* (Westport, Conn.: Greenwood Press, 1973).

9. Although regrettably little scholarship studies Joel A. Rogers specifically, he was an extremely influential voice in black America during the 1930s. His reporting from and about Africa struck a chord in black America. Indeed, Robert A. Hill argues that Rogers's reports from Africa and his regular column of African diasporic history, serialized in the *Pittsburgh Courier,* can be credited for that newspaper's increased circulation in the 1930s. See Robert A. Hill and R. Kent Rasmussen, "Afterward," *Black Empire* (Boston: Northeastern University Press, 1991), 259–325.

10. Donald N. Levine, *Greater Ethiopia: The Evolution of a Multiethnic Society* (Chicago: University of Chicago Press, 1974).

11. Henderson Braddick, "A New Look at American Policy during the Italo-Ethiopian Crisis, 1935–36," *Journal of Modern History* 34.1 (1962): 64–73.

12. Alberto Sbacchi, *Legacy of Bitterness: Ethiopia and Fascist Italy, 1935–1941* (Lawrenceville, N.J.: Red Sea Press, 1997).

13. Cedric J. Robinson, "Fascism and the Intersections of Capitalism, Racialism, and Historical Consciousness," *Humanities in Society* 6 (1983): 327.

14. Harris, *African-American Reactions,* 41.

15. Cited in Rodney Anson Ross, "Black Americans and Haiti, Liberia, the Virgin Islands, and Ethiopia, 1929–1936" (PhD diss., University of Chicago, 1975).

16. William Watts Chaplin, *Blood and Ink: An Italo-Ethiopian War Diary* (New York: Telegraph Press, 1936); Mortimer Durand, *Crazy Campaign: A Personal Narrative of the Italo-Abyssinian War* (London: G. Routledge, 1936).

17. Gordon MacCreagh, *The Last of Free Africa* (New York: The Century Co., 1928).

18. Harris, *African-American Reactions.*

19. Weisbord, *Ebony Kinship.*

20. Carleton S. Coon, "A Realist Looks at Ethiopia," *Atlantic Monthly* 156.3 (1935): 310–15. Indeed, this critique continues to surface in popular and academic appraisals of black America's relationship with Africa, although, in the colonial context of the interwar period it was, perhaps, motivated by a more pressing political anxiety.

21. Scott, *Sons of Sheba's Race,* 192.

22. Carter G. Woodson and Arthur Schomburg, for example, articulated academic arguments about black history intended to combat prominent theories of black America's absence from history and to provide a framework for the development of a black American nationality. The Negro History Movement confronted a racial edifice in which black America's absence in the historical record ostensibly evidenced an absence of agency in the present. Woodson, Schomburg, and others explored the potential of scholarly discourse to facilitate social change. Rogers's work evolved in concert with developments in the academic study of black history and life. Academic historians affiliated with the Association for the Study of Afro-American Life and History explored the progressive efficacy of motivated historical scholarship and appreciations of Africa free from the assumptions of white supremacy.

23. George Wells Parker, *Children of the Sun* (Baltimore: Black Classic Press, 1981); Hubert Harrison, *When Africa Awakes* (Baltimore: Black Classic Press, 1996).

24. Myrtle Pollard, "Harlem as Is" (New York: City College of New York, 1937), 33.

25. Roi Ottley, *New World a-Coming.*

26. Joel Augustus Rogers, *The Real Facts about Ethiopia* ([1936]; repr., Baltimore: Black Classic Press, 1982), 5.

27. Rogers, *The Real Facts,* 5.

28. Ibid., 5, 29.

29. Ibid., 17, 7.

30. W. E. B. Du Bois, "Inter-Racial Implications of the Ethiopian Crisis: A Negro View," in *Writings by W. E. B. Du Bois in Periodicals Edited by Others,* vol. 3: *1935–1944* (Milwood, N.Y.: Kraus-Thomson Limited, 1982).

31. Du Bois, "Inter-Racial Implications of the Ethiopian Crisis: A Negro View," 15.

32. Kirt H. Wilson, "Towards a Discursive Theory of Racial Identity: *The Souls of Black Folk* as a Response to Nineteenth Century Biological Determinism," *Western Journal of Communication* 63.2 (1999): 193–215.

33. Du Bois, "Inter-Racial Implications of the Ethiopian Crisis," 16.

34. Early in his public career, Du Bois understood the social categories of "race" as being a function of relationships created and lived by human beings. However, as his thought matured, he became increasingly concerned with economic conditions, the distribution of resources, and how political economy influenced the

relationships that create categories of people. He made this connection between discursive and economic reasons for "race" clearly in his analysis of the causes of a 1917 race riot in St. Louis; W. E. B. Du Bois, "Of Work and Wealth," in *Darkwater: Voices from within the Veil* (New York: Dover, 1999), 47–59.

35. Du Bois, "Inter-Racial Implications of the Ethiopian Crisis," 18.

36. Matthew Pratt Guterl, *The Color of Race in America, 1900–1940* (Cambridge, Mass.: Harvard University Press, 2001).

37. Lothrop Theodore Stoddard, *The Rising Tide of Color against White World Supremacy* (New York: C. Scribner's Sons, 1920).

38. Cited in Scott *Sons of Sheba's Race,* 121.

39. Ibid., 123.

40. Mark Lawrence McPhail, "From Complicity to Coherence: Rereading the Rhetoric of Afrocentricity," *Western Journal of Communication* 62 (1998): 115.

41. See David Theo Goldberg, *Racist Culture: Philosophy and the Politics of Meaning* (Cambridge, Mass.: Blackwell, 1993).

42. Victoria Gallagher makes a similar argument about Stokely Carmichael's "Black Power" speech, asserting that Carmichael's speech views American racial politics through the lens of black America's experience and thus inverts the racist logic operating in the rhetoric of white supremacy and that of well-intentioned white liberals. See Victoria J. Gallagher, "Black Power in Berkeley: Postmodern Constructions in the Rhetoric of Stokely Carmichael," *Quarterly Journal of Speech* 87 (2001): 144–58.

43. Kirt H. Wilson, "Is There Interest in Reconciliation?" *Rhetoric and Public Affairs* 7 (2004): 370.

44. Rogers, *The Real Facts,* 8.

45. Ibid., 19, 21.

46. Ibid., 22, 8, 14.

47. Ibid., 24, 28–29.

48. Ibid., 2.

49. Walter White, *New York Amsterdam News,* October 5, 1935, Editorial sec., 15.

50. As Bonnie Barthold argues, cyclical time creates tremendous responsibility for a community to maintain this temporal cycle, but it also implies the agency with which to do so. In a premodern sense of cyclical time, communities must act in accordance with the requirements of the cycle. For example, in Chinua Achebe's *Things Fall Apart,* Okonkwo's violation of the Week of Peace jeopardizes the community's purchase on the present and disrupts the faith that the cycle will maintain. Thus, as Bruce Davison argues in *The African Genius,* a cyclical sense of time "taught the supremacy of man in controlling or influencing his own present or future. Far from imposing a grim subjection to blind forces of nature, it held to a shrewd realism . . . it is mankind that matters — meaning, in this context, that any man can always be responsible for himself" (p. 146). See Bonnie Barthold, *Black Time: Fiction of Africa, the Caribbean, and the United States* (New Haven: Yale University Press, 1981); Basil Davidson, *The African Genius* (Akron: Ohio University Press, 2004).

51. Pierre Nora, "Between Memory and History: Les Lieux de Mémoire," in *History and Memory in African American Culture*, ed. Robert O'Meally and Genevieve Fabre (Oxford: Oxford University Press, 1994), 286.

52. Nora, "Between Memory and History," 286. See also Michel De Certeau, *The Writing of History* (New York: Columbia University Press, 1988).

53. Genevieve Fabre, "African American Commemorative Celebrations in the Nineteenth Century," in *History and Memory in African American Culture*, ed. Robert O'Meally and Genevieve Fabre (Oxford: Oxford University Press, 1994), 73.

54. See Genevieve Fabre and Robert O'Meally, eds., *History and Memory in African American Culture*.

55. Elizabeth Rauh Bethel, "Images of Hayti: The Construction of an Afro-American Lieu de Mémoire," *Callaloo* 15 (1992): 827–41.

56. Cited in Harris, *African-Americans Reactions*, 44.

57. Scott, *Sons of Sheba's Race*, 50.

58. Cited in Scott, *Sons of Sheba's Race*, 123.

59. Bernard Magubane, *The Ties That Bind: African-American Consciousness of Africa* (Trenton, N.J.: Africa World Press, 1987), 160.

6. Anticolonial Rhetoric and Black Civil Rights History

1. See "God Help Africa," *Time*, July 29, 1935, 31; Roi Ottley, *New World a-Coming* (Boston: Houghton Mifflin, 1943).

2. Stuart Hall, "Cultural Identity and Diaspora," in *Identity: Community, Culture, Difference*, ed. Jonathan Rutherford (London: Lawrence & Wishart, 1990), 227.

3. Madison Grant, *The Passing of the Great Race; or, the Racial Basis of European History* (New York: C. Scribner, 1916).

4. Stephanie Batiste, "Epaulettes and Leaf Skirts, Warriors and Subversives: Black National Subjectivity in Macbeth and Haiti," *Text and Performance Quarterly* 23.2 (2003): 154–85.

5. "Julian: Black Eagle Preens Self for Flight to Aden, Abyssinia," *Newsweek*, September 30, 1933, 32, 34; Morris Markey, "The Black Eagle—I," *The New Yorker*, July 11, 1931, 22–25; Henry Lee Moon, *The Black Eagle Flops*, Editorial digest and manuscript file 35, 1936, Arthur A. Schomburg Center for Research in Black Culture, New York City Public Library.

6. Daniel Aldridge, "A War for the Colored Races: Anti-Interventionism and the African American Intelligentsia, 1939–1941," *Diplomatic History* 28.3 (2004): 328.

7. Danny Duncan Collum and Victor A. Berch, eds., *African Americans in the Spanish Civil War: "This Ain't Ethiopia, But It'll Do"* (New York: G. K. Hall, 1992).

8. Joseph E. Harris, *African-Americans' Reactions to War in Ethiopia, 1936–1941* (Baton Rouge: Louisiana State University Press, 1994).

9. James A. Meriwether, *Proudly We Can Be Africans: Black Americans and Africa, 1935–1961* (Chapel Hill: University of North Carolina Press, 2002).

10. Celeste Condit and John Lucaites, *Crafting Equality: America's Anglo-African Word* (Chicago: University of Chicago Press, 1993).

11. Divine and Grace founded communes that applied popular New Thought mysticism to domestic social problems. See Jill Watts, *God, Harlem, U.S.A.: The Father Divine Story* (Berkeley: University of California Press, 1992).

12. Marcus Garvey, "The Smell of Mussolini," in *The Marcus Garvey and Universal Negro Improvement Association Papers, November 1927–August 1940,* ed. Robert A. Hill (Berkeley: University of California Press, 1990), 642.

13. Marcus Garvey, *The Marcus Garvey and Universal Negro Improvement Association Papers, November 1927–August 1940,* ed. Robert A. Hill (Berkeley: University of California Press, 1990), 740.

14. "Mr. Garvey without Genuine Racial Attachment," *The Voice of Ethiopia,* February 17, 1937, 1–2; Malaku Bayen, "Is Marcus Garvey Faithful to Himself?" *Voice of Ethiopia,* January 1937.

15. Colin Grant, *Negro with a Hat: The Rise and Fall of Marcus Garvey* (Oxford: Oxford University Press, 2008).

16. Michael W. Fitzgerald, "'We Have Found a Moses': Theodore Bilbo, Black Nationalism, and the Greater Liberia Bill of 1939," *Journal of Southern History* 63.2 (1997): 293–320.

17. Brenda Gayle Plummer, *Rising Wind: Black Americans and U.S. Foreign Affairs, 1935–1960* (Chapel Hill: University of North Carolina Press, 1996), 107.

18. James H. Meriwether, *Proudly We Can Be Africans: Black America and Africa, 1935–1961* (Chapel Hill: North Carolina Press, 2002), 68.

19. James L. Roark, "American Black Leaders: The Response to Colonialism and the Cold War, 1943–1953," *African Historical Studies* 4.2 (1971): 253.

20. Meriwether, *Proudly We Can Be Africans,* 59.

21. John Lewis Gaddis, *The United States and the Origin of the Cold War, 1941–47* (New York: Columbia University Press, 2000), 352.

22. Roark, "American Black Leaders," 259.

23. Cited in Roark, "American Black Leaders," 260.

24. Melvin Tolson, "Quotes or Unquotes on Poetry," *Kansas Quarterly* 7 (1975): 37.

25. Melvin Tolson, *Harlem Gallery and Other Poems of Melvin B. Tolson,* ed. Raymond Nelson with an introduction by Rita Dove (Charlottesville: University of Virginia Press, 1999), 163.

26. Robin D. G. Kelly, *Freedom Dreams: The Black Radical Imagination* (Boston: Beacon, 2002).

27. George Schuyler, *Black Empire* (Boston: Northeastern University Press, 1993).

INDEX